India in Slow Motion

India in Slow Motion

MARK TULLY
and
GILLIAN WRIGHT

VIKING
an imprint of
PENGUIN BOOKS

VIKING

Published by the Penguin Group
Penguin Books Ltd, 80 Strand, London WC2R ORL, England
Penguin Putnam Inc., 375 Hudson Street, New York, New York 10014, USA
Penguin Books Australia Ltd, 250 Camberwell Road,
Camberwell, Victoria 3124, Australia
Penguin Books Canada Ltd, 10 Alcorn Avenue, Toronto, Ontario, Canada M4V 3B2
Penguin Books India (P) Ltd, 11 Community Centre,
Panchsheel Park, New Delhi – 110 017, India
Penguin Books (NZ) Ltd, Cnr Rosedale and Airborne Roads,
Albany, Auckland, New Zealand
Penguin Books (South Africa) (Pty) Ltd, 24 Sturdee Avenue,
Rosebank 2196, South Africa

Penguin Books Ltd, Registered Offices: 80 Strand, London WC2R ORL, England

www.penguin.com

First published 2002
1

Set in 12/14.75 Monotype Bembo
Typeset by Intype London Ltd
Printed in Great Britain by Clays Ltd, St Ives plc

A CIP catalogue record for this book is available from the British Library

ISBN 0–6708–8558–4

To all those who are striving
for the good of India

Contents

Acknowledgements

We would like to thank all those who have helped us during our travels for this book, especially I. B. Singh, Madhukar Shah of Orcha, Mario Miranda and his family, Percival Naronha, Frederick Naronha, Claud Alvares, G. S. Radhakrishna, Uday Mahurkar, Yusuf Jameel, Pushkar Johari, all those who gave us their time on our travels, and the team in our home in Delhi – Ravi Prasad Narayanan in the office, and Ram Chander and Bubbly in the kitchen.

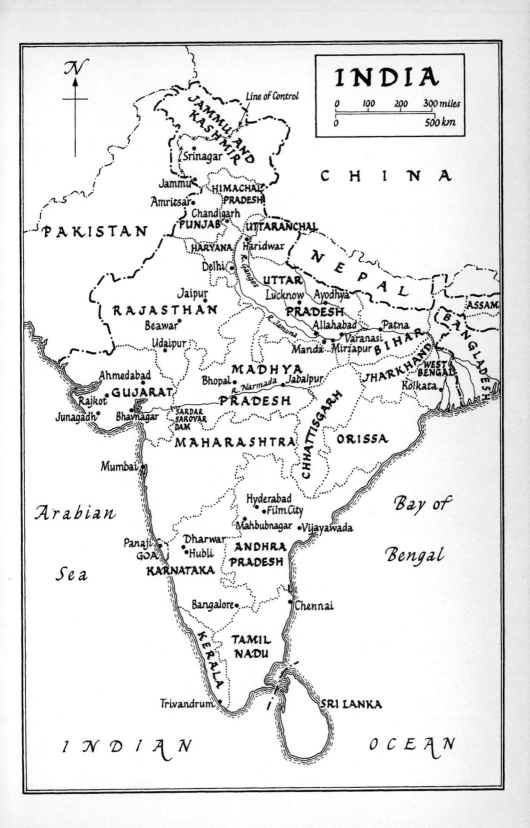

Introduction

Not a word passed between them as they strode towards the town of Orcha with its temples to visit and its sacred river to bathe in. These were peaceful pilgrims, they carried peacock feathers as standards and sticks for dancing, not for doing battle. They were robed for rejoicing, with cowbells tinkling on their cross-belts, while round their waists gaudy green and red pom-poms bounced. Some wore vests embroidered with rosettes, and some pointed multicoloured clowns' hats. There would have been loud praising of their gods too had this not been the end of a week of abstinence when not a word was to be spoken. The men of the villages of Bundelkhand, a region of central India, were on their way to celebrate one of their immemorial festivals when their silence was broken by the wail of a siren. An inspector of police in khaki uniform clutching the handle of his motorbike in one hand and imperiously waving everyone off the road with the other appeared round the corner. He was followed by a white car with a blue light revolving on the roof and one star above black number plates, the badge of office of a deputy inspector general of police. The convoy, completed by a pick-up full of armed policemen, hurtled past, scattering the pilgrims in a cloud of dust. They couldn't see whether the superintendent of police, the representative of the Raj which succeeded the British, even bothered to glance at their discomfiture shielded as he was from those he ruled by firmly closed, heavily tinted windows. Waiting in our car to pass the pilgrims I was reminded of the senior Indian civil servant who had said to me, 'Our police are only for the poor. They don't touch the rich and the influential.'

We were on our way to see a cyber-café that a non-governmental organization had set up in a remote village. There we were told that the computers had been much more useful when they could pull down material from a satellite. But then some bureaucrat had discovered that the NGO needed an Internet Service Provider Licence II and had ordered them to dismantle the aerials. The government itself had proved quite unable to provide any connection with the outside world. There was a wireless mast for one public telephone but the villagers said no one had come to maintain the battery for years. The villagers themselves were of course not allowed to touch government property. As I have found so often in India the government was the problem not the solution.

The police officer with his convoy, and the bureaucrats who ordered the aerials to be dismantled, were the unchanging India, the India which is still shackled by a colonial bureaucracy, the India which has become a byword for red-tape and corruption, the India described by one of its most distinguished civil servants as a kleptocracy. This was the India that, according to a recent World Bank report, still has social indicators that are 'poor by most measures of human development'. But there is a changing India too. In the same report the World Bank also said that India's economy had, since the 1980s, been among the fastest growing in the world. Indian democracy has brought about a social revolution. The lower castes, because they are largest in number, have come to dominate the political scene. There is a sophisticated Indian elite and a sizeable well-educated middle class: thoroughly professional lawyers, bankers and accountants, academics, engineers, doctors, all admired by their peers in other parts of the world. India is renowned for its information technology skills. Civil society is vibrant, India has become the NGO capital of the world. Television has grown from a drab purveyor of government propaganda to a multi-channel independent media. The press, once obsessed with politics, now provides news and a bewildering variety of views on every aspect of Indian life, including the misdeeds of those who wield power.

Why then is India still in slow motion? Part of the answer lies in this story from the Indian Institute of Technology in Delhi, or IIT, a symbol of modern India's potential – a first-class university, teaching the cream of India's science students. Rukmini Bhaya Nair is an effervescent enthusiast for the humanities, charged with persuading IIT students that there is more to knowledge than just science and technology. Apparently, if she travels on official business she is asked to fill in a form on which she can still claim for travelling by camel, or canal, depending on the version. The small print also sets out the rules for claiming second-class fare (without meals) on steamers, and mentions the furlongs travelled by trolley. What about more modern forms of travel? According to Rukmini Bhaya Nair: 'Our clerks of the government of India have simply added air-travel to the list of possible conveyances – a final palimpsest layer.' And what conclusion does she draw from this? 'Despite our flirtation with the latest computer technology, our gleaming machines, and the constant talk of efficiency, we at the hi-tech IIT remain the hostages of history. The obfuscatory rites of colonial administration are with us still and everyone is caught equally helplessly in the toils of the paper chase.' Those obfuscatory rites would have been done away with if politicians had concentrated on the most obvious issue facing India – bad governance. That would go against their own vested interests so they have distracted the voters' attention by raising issues of caste and creed.

There have been many explanations for the failures of India. Some centre on India's past, its history of invasions and foreign domination – Naipaul has described it as a wounded civilization. Some blame India's culture, and its religions, seeing it as a land of fatalism, a society set in stone by the caste system. Some even blame the climate, saying it has sapped the will of the people. These explanations denigrate India, Indians, and an ancient culture that has been described by the poet Kathleen Raine as 'having more fully than any other civilization on earth, past or present, explored and embodied the highest and the most embracing realization of our human scope'. It is these critiques that are fatalistic for they suggest that there is nothing that can be done, the flaws are fatal and India is fated to be a poor and backward country.

In this book we argue that one of the fundamental problems of India is a peculiarly Indian form of bad governance. The need to do something about governance was acknowledged by the Prime Minister of India, Atal Behari Vajpayee when he addressed the

the police to do except reunite children with their parents. Tolerant Hinduism had triumphed.

But as we had our last cup of tea on the verandah of Kanak Bhavan's guest house, Ajai returned to the subject of tolerance which was clearly bothering him. 'You know,' he said, 'I bought a Bible and a Qur'an and I found no religion teaches violence, but still I do think Hindus' peaceful nature has always been exploited by fanatics.' I didn't want to argue with him, or remind him that it was Hindus who were threatening the peace of Ayodhya, with their warrior Rama. No one could be less aggressive than Ajai or more peace-loving, yet even he had been influenced by the Rama who seeks revenge. The festival had confirmed our belief that in spite of the destruction of the mosque and the BJP coming to power in Delhi for the first time, Hindu fundamentalism was not sweeping the country; but we had come to realize how insidious creating a sense of grievance could be.

Misplaced Charity

Mirzapur stands on the banks of the Ganges, overshadowed by two neighbours. Varanasi or Benares, Shiva's city, is downriver, and upriver to the west is Allahabad where every twelve years, when the stars come together in a particularly auspicious association, millions and millions of Hindus gather for the Kumbh Mela and bathe at the point where the Ganges meets Delhi's river, the Jamuna. But I believe on the festival of Diwali in the year 2000, Mirzapur outshone both its neighbours.

Diwali is the festival of lights. In northern India it celebrates the joyous return of the warrior king and god Rama after rescuing his wife, Sita, from the demon ruler of Lanka. On the evening of Diwali 2000 in Mirzapur an armada of *diyas*, or traditional lamps, set sail on the Ganges to welcome Rama and Sita home. Standing in the darkness on a cliff high above the river, as one of many guests at a Diwali party, I saw first a pinpoint of light float slowly downstream. It was soon followed by another, and another, until the flames flickering in the clay saucers became a Milky Way on the dark waters of the Ganges. Lamps were still being launched as the vanguard of the armada disappeared round the distant bend in the river.

When the last lamp had sailed past us a torch flashed from the river, and somewhere from the clifftop a reply was sent. Inevitably there followed much shouting from the river and the cliff before fifteen boatmen from the Mallah, or fishermen, caste scrambled up a steep path to join us. They had launched the fleet, but the review had been organized by our host Edward Oakley, chairman of the Mirzapur-based carpet company Obeetee, and for many years a member of the Mirzapur Club on whose lawn we were standing, and from where a regular supply of drinks flowed.

The tall, blonde wife of the American ambassador, carefully

casual in a stylish white kameez patterned with large red flowers in Moghul design, stood out from the rest of Edward's motley guests assembled on the clifftop. The host himself had made no sartorial concessions to his distinguished guests. He was dressed in trousers which fitted loosely round his enormous girth, a shirt, and braces clearly visible to all. Edward was a large man. With his rubicund face, head fringed by just a thin strip of closely clipped grey hair above what can only be called a bull neck, he reminded me of the pictures of Edward VII seen on cigar packets. Speaking basic Hindustani with an almost deliberately English accent, inheritor of a business founded by his father during the Raj, upholder of the British tradition of the burra peg or large whisky, and accompanied usually by his faithful factotum, Bhagwan Das, Edward Oakley could all too easily be taken as a caricature of someone who had 'stayed on', a relic of the Raj. In fact he was an extremely astute businessman who had converted his father's somewhat ramshackle business into what an American carpet designer once told me was the most efficient and quality conscious manufacturer he had ever come across.

The headquarters of Obeetee were just across the road from the club in the spacious compound of what had been Edward's parents' home. We were to dine that night in the burra or big bungalow, now the company guest house. But before we left the river, Edward called for a group photo, and announced that he would sit in front on the ground with the Mallahs.

'Yes,' piped up Bhagwan Das, 'but how will you get up?'

Edward's voice boomed, 'With your help. After all it was you who organized this whole *tamasha*.'

That was certainly true. Edward never tired of acknowledging his dependence on Bhagwan Das, often saying that he should run Obeetee. Between the two men there was what seemed to me the close relationship of a master and a faithful servant. Edward put it differently.

'When Bhagwan Das is not around I get into trouble. When he arrives on the scene he gets me out of trouble, and when he is with me he ensures that I do not get into trouble, and what is more, he thinks for me both at home and in business. He is my thoroughly modern Jeeves.'

As we were assembling for the photo, there was a slight hiccough when I asked the boatmen how many lamps there were. The Hindi word for lamp is very similar to the past participle of the verb to give and the boatmen, thinking I had asked how much money they'd been given said, somewhat aggressively, 'We haven't discussed that yet.' Bhagwan Das rescued me, making my meaning clear, and the Mallahs told me they had launched a thousand lamps from their boats.

Sitting on the verandah of the big bungalow having yet more drinks, the American ambassador explained how his wife's interest in carpets had led to their friendship with Edward. The Diwali party would have been an opportunity for Edward to lobby the ambassador about the threat to his sales in America from a campaign against child labour mounted by the Rugmark Foundation. But Edward considered this would be rather tasteless.

The Foundation was attracting US importers by stating on its website that 'The Rugmark label guarantees the carpet was not made by children' and that 'Through Rugmark's media campaign your company will be highlighted in the national news as an importer of child-labor-free carpets.' Though elsewhere on the website Rugmark's claims for its label were diluted to 'the best assurance that a child's fingers will not weave the carpets you import', Edward felt that the impression was being created that Rugmark was promising something it couldn't deliver. Carpets are a cottage industry, woven in looms scattered over thousands of villages, which makes inspection very difficult. Edward has argued that there isn't an inspection scheme which can guarantee that no child has worked on any labelled carpet. He is afraid that if any Rugmark manufacturers are exposed as using child labour, it could have a disastrous impact on every company whose carpets carry the label. His company had paid a price for rejecting the Rugmark label, losing their market in Germany, the largest European carpet importer. The foundation was launched there with the support of the German government, and had now turned its attention to the United States, Obeetee's main market.

Edward was a natural raconteur of the self-deprecatory tradition nurtured in British public schools. His career at his father's old school, Rossall in the north of England, had apparently 'not been entirely satisfactory' and he'd left as soon as possible to be articled to a chartered accountant. He'd chosen that profession because all the accountants he'd met had seemed to be 'thickies', and so he thought the profession would suit him.

He scraped through his intermediate exam first time, but then, Edward explained, there came a setback in his career. 'For the next two years I considered passing such an achievement that I didn't do any study whatsoever. I gambled on the horses and cards and had a jolly good time. The first time I took the finals I failed.'

Edward guffawed, and we all laughed too, including the ambassador, who, although he gave me the impression of a man who had never failed at anything in his life, was greatly enjoying Edward's story.

'Of course, my father didn't think it was quite so funny,' Edward went on. 'He was out here in Mirzapur and he proceeded to turn my photograph on the mantelpiece around to face the wall and I was in disgrace. But my mother turned the picture round and I took the exam again and passed. I don't know how.'

White uniformed, bare-footed servants, under the ever-watchful eye of Bhagwan Das, ensured no glass was empty. Punkahs turned lazily, more to disturb the flight plans of the mosquitoes than to provide relief from the temperature, which was quite comfortable that night. But there was no sign of dinner. I didn't mind, having reached the stage when I didn't want dinner to interfere with the drinking. Nor did Edward, who continued his story.

Apparently, Edward's joining of his father's business had not been planned. He came to Mirzapur on holiday from the London accountancy firm where he was working. It was the first time he'd been back since he left as a child and he was bowled over by the bungalow and its magnificent, manicured garden. He thought to himself, 'Edward, this is going to be like early retirement to come to Mirzapur, and no more of that ticking trade called accountancy.'

Another Englishman in the party who had stayed on in Mirzapur too, and was still running a small carpet firm, said, 'Come on, Edward, you didn't just sit on your backside. You really gave the old firm a good shaking. What about the day you burnt all the files?'

'Well,' replied Edward laughing again, 'I was a great admirer of my father and he taught me everything about this business. But I was young and I did think there were some rather strange things which could be improved. One was Afaq Ahmad, who was meant to tell me about the progress made on any order. He had a straggly beard, looked like somebody out of the Bible. So rather than a Pharisee, I called him a scribe, because he always had a pen and his fingers were covered with ink. When I asked him what the position was with a carpet he would say with great confidence, six feet had been woven, the next day he would tell me with equal confidence that nothing had been woven. Amusing maybe, but not to our buyer in New York who was wanting to cancel his order.'

One day an infuriated Edward had summoned the scribe and ordered him to hand over all his records to a peon who had dumped them in the boiler. 'After that,' Edward said, 'Mr Afaq had another job and life became a lot easier.'

Edward had also cleared out the design room in the factory where thousands and thousands of old carpet designs were kept suspended precariously in wire netting over the heads of the designers. Edward's father, who apparently was 'not a throw away person', had refused to let him burn the designs, and so he hired four bullock carts to carry them from the factory back to the compound in Mirzapur. 'My father and his partner were quite shocked,' Edward said, 'but that was the end of the designs.'

It was well past ten o'clock and the *diyas* lining the paths of the Obeetee compound were burnt out when Edward finished his stories and led us into the main room of the burra bungalow. Separate tables for four were laid out on the polished wooden floor. The vast room with its sparse, dark, colonial-style furniture, its faded antique rugs, and its fireplace would have changed little since Edward's parents lived there.

The dinner opened with soup followed by fish and chips, but moved from there to tandoori chicken and other Indian dishes. As soon as dinner was over the ambassador and his wife retired to the best bedroom in the bungalow and the rest of the guests dispersed. This was not discourteous but just normal practice in India today – drink hard, eat late and then leave.

Mirzapur had not yet gone to sleep. As we drove back to the Hotel Galaxy, which had none of the old world charm of the bungalow, in fact it had no charm at all, children threw crackers under our car, stalls selling small clay images of Lakshmi and the elephant god Ganesh were still open, and sweet-makers were bawling their bargain prices over loudspeakers. Our driver said, 'They must be duplicate. You can't make pure milk sweets for that money.'

Carpet making is the backbone of the economy of a vast region centred on Mirzapur. It's an industry with a long history. In the late 1830s Emily Eden, travelling up the Ganges with her brother Lord Auckland who was the Governor General, noted in her diary, 'We made an expedition to Mirzapur the great carpet manufactory.' Unfortunately she did not describe the manufacturing process but it seems unlikely that the weaving would have been markedly different from today.

The looms are still heavy wooden beams round which the cotton threads of the warp are stretched. The weavers sit in a pit behind the loom, tying knot after knot, each one marked by a dot on the *naqsha*, or map of the carpet. The ill-lit sheds in which most weavers work have probably not changed that much either. But the finishing processes have. To a first-time observer, it's a miracle that those processes don't finish the carpet.

In the washery, the back of the intricate floor coverings the villagers have toiled so long at their looms to weave are first singed with a blowlamp. As if that wasn't hazardous enough, they are then doused in a series of baths with different strong chemicals which can all too easily discolour them if not applied in correct proportions.

After each bath the sodden wool is pummelled by wooden paddles until most of the water has oozed out. When at last the bathing and bashing is completed the bedraggled carpet is laid out in the sun to dry.

The washing, and the more intricate finishing that takes place afterwards, are labour intensive, a vital employer in one of India's poorest regions. Edward believes that shock publicity, if it leads those in the developed world to believe that all Indian carpets other than those endorsed by Rugmark are the product of child labour, is a threat to this industry, which is one of the very few in India that puts money into the villages. Other traditional manufacturers like potters, cloth weavers, shoe and soap makers have been driven out of business by modern machinery, forcing millions to leave their villages and swell the slums of the large cities.

Before we'd left Delhi, another Englishman involved in the carpet industry, who agreed with Edward's assessment of Rugmark, had come to have lunch with us. Robin Garland had once been chief executive of Scottish Heritage, a group which owned E. Hill and Company, Obeetee's traditional rivals. When he was accused by the British press of employing child weavers, he admitted he didn't know whether that was so and promised to go to India to see for himself. On that visit he decided education was the main problem. Because there were no schools worth the name, children had no alternative but to work on the looms. He founded a non-governmental organization called Project Mala which had established schools in the carpet belt.

Although Robin now spent all his time on Project Mala, he still looked like a businessman with his pink shirt, and tie – only obligatory in Delhi's business and diplomatic communities – his expensive shining black slip-ons and his neatly cut grey hair. He was a rich man, a millionaire, but he did say, 'only a small one now'.

I asked him, 'How does an efficient businessman like you cope with all the inefficiencies of India?'

His bright blue eyes softened, and he gave one of his rare smiles. 'Sometimes you don't. The other day I told an official of the education ministry that many of the government schools did not have teachers or pupils. He accepted that but when I suggested that Project Mala should take over some of the schools and run them he replied, "Oh, we couldn't possibly abdicate our responsibility for education." That's the bureaucracy for you. Not exactly logical.'

In India words often don't mean quite what they appear to mean, and the carpet industry is no exception. A carpet manufacturer usually has no role in the manufacture of the carpet, the weaving. He gets the orders, supplies the wool and the design, and finishes the carpet when it comes off the loom. But the weavers are employed by a loom owner, often a weaver himself, and most of the manufacturers Rugmark deals with don't have any contact with them. They deal through a middleman, a contractor. So the manufacturer can be two stages removed from the looms yet he is the person who guarantees to Rugmark that no children are working on them.

Robin had seen a recent television documentary on Channel 4 called *Slavery* which had shown the ethical director of B&Q, a major British retailer, advocating Rugmark. Robin said, 'I let him know what I thought of his ethics. I told him, "You are having the wool pulled over your eyes. You are buying Rugmark carpets from an exporter who doesn't have any looms of his own. How can he know whether they are genuinely child-labour-free?" I told the director straight.' He added, 'I'm a blunt Yorkshireman. I'm not known for my tact.'

Perhaps, not surprisingly, Robin Garland's man on the spot, David Rangpal, was not an enthusiast for the labelling scheme. Driving out of Mirzapur to see one of the Mala schools, he told us that he had shocked a United Nations working group on child labour by telling one of their meetings in Geneva, 'Child labour as such is no problem in the carpet industry. The problem is lack of an alternative, and in particular lack of educational opportunities.'

David Rangpal, tall by Indian standards, white haired, soft spoken and sad faced, was a distinguished educationalist himself. A sociologist with an American Ph. D. and post-doctoral work at the School of Oriental and African Studies in London behind him, he had come back to the Punjab to head a Christian college. During the Sikh troubles, the separatist movement led by Sant Jarnail Singh

Bhindranwale in the eighties, he had narrowly escaped an attempt on his life. He and his wife had then both felt called to this educational backwater, to accept a meagre salary, and manage the Mala schools. We soon learned the reason for his sad expression. His wife had been killed in a car accident two years earlier. He said, 'I see in Project Mala my wife.' A devout Christian, he didn't worry what others thought of his work. 'I am not the judge,' he said, 'nor is anyone else. God is the judge, let him decide.'

However, David Rangpal did judge the government's efforts to provide education for the children of the carpet belt. His view was that the government was not competent to provide education or any other services. As we drove past a new large office block, with residential accommodation for staff, he peered out of the window shortsightedly and said, 'Take a look at that. It's a good example of the way the government functions, or doesn't function, I should say.'

He told the driver to stop and reverse so that we could get a better look and went on with remarkable bitterness for such a mild-mannered man: 'This is the new local government headquarters. The public have to come here for everything they want to get done, for all their needs, but they can't get here. It's in the middle of nowhere.' The complex was indeed set in the middle of a treeless, barren wasteland, miles from the nearest town.

A short distance ahead David stopped the car again and insisted that we got out to inspect a local health centre. The only sign of medicine we could see was a datura bush growing out of the dilapidated, deserted, building. There were two charpoys inside, evidence that it was occupied at night, and evidence on the floor that the accommodation was shared by cattle.

From there we proceeded to the small town of Marihan where we drove into a walled compound, with another crumbling concrete building at one side. 'This is the bus station, and that's the ticket office,' David said. 'But as you can see, no buses. They can't be bothered to come in here because it's easier to stop on the road.' We checked with the only government employee we could find, a watchman. He confirmed it was a bus station unvisited by buses.

'Everything is rotting away,' he said. 'This is the arrangement of the government.'

After Marihan, we turned down a road which ran along the banks of a canal, full of green water. The unhealthy colour didn't deter young boys from bathing. We learnt that the canal had been dry until farmers had blocked the road and forced the government to attend to their demand for irrigation – just in time to save the rice crop. At last we found a government school. There was no one to be seen. A notice chalked on a blackboard read 'Going to the Bank'.

When we reached the Project Mala school there was a full staff, classes in Hindi and environmental studies were underway, girls were learning to tailor school uniforms, and boys were sitting behind looms learning to weave. Signs on the wall advocated a mixture of health, hygiene, morality, and commonsense: 'Eat Green Vegetables', 'Weakness is the Biggest Sin', 'There is Strength in Unity', 'Keep Food Covered', 'Strength Without Wisdom is in Vain'. We shared an excellent lunch of *khichri*, spinach, and raw white radishes, with the girls and boys dressed in uniform dark-blue checked shirts worn outside sky-blue trousers. They sat in orderly lines cross-legged on the floor. A brief grace, appropriate to any religion, was said before lunch, 'Oh, God bless this food, and we thank you for this meal.'

After lunch the children poured out of the whitewashed concrete school into the playground at the front surrounded by roses, and purple bougainvilleas. Impromptu games of football and other sports broke out. Gilly persuaded some of the boys to surrender part of their break and be interviewed. Only one said that he did work on a loom at home but maintained his father was very keen that he should continue his education. David explained that much of the confusion about child labour was caused by a failure to differentiate between bonded, or slave labour, children working for wages on looms near their homes, and children who helped their families to weave carpets. 'So much of the publicity,' he said, 'gives the impression that every child working on a loom is a slave.'

Several years earlier we had seen slave children. There were six of them, all seemed about ten years old, weaving on a loom in a village some distance from Mirzapur. Clothes hung on pegs on the wall behind them. Their bedding rolls, and a pile of tin plates showed quite clearly that the boys ate and slept in the shed where they worked. They were too frightened to talk. We were taken to that weaving shed by volunteers working with Champa Devi, a woman who practised what most Indians unfortunately now regard as the outdated virtues of Mahatma Gandhi.

We found Champa Devi again, still wearing a sari woven from hand-spun cotton, the Gandhian material known as *khadi*, and still working from her small house facing a noisy, narrow street in the heart of Mirzapur. The walls of the front room, which doubled as her office, were lined with the legal books of her husband. I remembered him telling us that he never got time to attend to his own practice because he was so busy fighting cases brought by his wife on behalf of slave children or their parents, so I asked whether that was still so. Tears welled up behind the spectacles of the diminutive fighter for children's rights – she must have been well under five feet – the white, blue-bordered sari was adjusted to ensure it covered all her hair – and she replied, 'My husband died just before my daughter's wedding, so we had to have the funeral and the wedding. It was hard to bear. You knew him, he was a good man.'

All we could mumble was, 'Yes.'

Champa Devi had been working for the release and welfare of bonded labour since 1973. All her workers were volunteers, and quite a few of them were crammed into that small room. When we last met her, she had been concentrating on releasing slave children and bringing cases on their behalf against their owners. But now she seemed less confident about that course of action. Staring directly at us, with her lips pursed grimly she said, 'I got two thousand two hundred people released, many of them were adult bonded labourers, but they are not insects that fly against the lights at night and can be swept away dead in the morning.'

One of Champa Devi's volunteers, making full use of tortuous legal terminology, tried to get us to understand how difficult it had been to get the police and the courts to interpret the legislation against child labour in their favour, but Champa Devi stopped him in his tracks. 'Don't start another meeting,' she said sharply, and then went on, 'as I said, I had those children released but now they are bonded again because they have no money. Without the help of the government I got them released but what will they eat if the government doesn't do anything for them after that?'

Champa Devi was also critical of other NGOs, especially those conducting raids to release slave children. 'After twenty years of releasing children I have to say I don't consider raids necessary. Publishing photos in the paper, that is not the answer.'

She would not name the publicity seekers, but we both knew who she meant.

When we came to Rugmark, Champa Devi was prepared to be specific. Pursing her lips even more tightly, and frowning, she launched into a diatribe against the foundation's practice of charging a percentage of the carpet's value from both exporters and importers who use the Rugmark label.

'Rugmark charges two per cent from the carpet people, and then what is the use of it if it can't get to the root cause of the bonded labour? It is certainly not our aim to collect money from the industry. What do they think, that you can stop slavery by centring your attention on money?'

When I pointed out that Rugmark spent much of the money it collected on rehabilitation and education she became even more incensed. 'If there is no rehabilitation for the family of the released boy then what will happen? Everything will be in vain unless the family is rehabilitated in a real sense. By putting twenty-five children in school will tens of millions of people be fed?' she ended scornfully.

We left Champa Devi to her battle with the government, which was refusing to take the problem of rehabilitation seriously, a losing battle, I couldn't help feeling.

As Champa Devi was no longer involved in releasing child slaves, we drove out of Mirzapur early the next morning to find a young man who was. We had been assured that he knew of villages where children were employed on looms. Crossing the bridge over the

Ganges, we drove on to the Grand Trunk Road which connects Calcutta with Delhi. In the time of Kipling's young hero Kim, the Grand Trunk Road used to run on to Lahore in what is now Pakistan. In those days it was 'a broad smiling river of life'. Kim found 'new people and new sights at every stride . . . here and there he met or was overtaken by the gaily dressed crowds of whole villages turning out to some local fair'.

We were on the road before the noxious river of modern life was in full flow. The trucks were still parked outside *dhabas*, the Indian equivalent of transport cafés, which also supply rudimentary accommodation. Many of their drivers were still asleep on charpoys, but the earlier risers were soaping themselves under hand-pumps, or reading the papers and discussing the news.

We drove for many miles before finding a dhaba with a really long line of trucks parked outside it – the more the trucks, the better the dhaba, is a rule of the Indian road. As we were waiting for our strong, sweet tea we casually enquired how far Meja was. It was the town where we were to turn off and drive into what is known as 'the interior'.

'Meja?' came back the surprised reply. 'You are on the wrong side of the Ganges. It's on the road which runs along the south bank, not this one.' Several drivers confirmed that we would have to go all the way back to Mirzapur and cross the river again there.

That wasn't the only delay we suffered. Once we had penetrated the interior we came across a line of traffic held up by a roadblock. This was a *chakka* or wheel jam. Redundant workers of a defunct spinning mill, owned by the Uttar Pradesh government, were protesting. The magic word 'journalist' didn't help – they weren't letting anyone pass. So we went in search of the office where negotiations were taking place.

It was set in a vast campus with spacious bungalows for the more senior staff. Their gardens were running to seed, and there was no sign of any industrial activity. Inside the office we found two police officers negotiating with trade union leaders. Everyone was very polite. The senior policeman, a short, stout young man from the elite cadre of the Uttar Pradesh state police, left most of the talking to his junior who was in charge of the local police station. The union leaders maintained that the commitments made by the government when the mill was closed had not been fulfilled. The final straw had been the visit of an accounts officer from the headquarters of the Uttar Pradesh Spinning Corporation, three of whose four mills were defunct. He had sold off waste from the factory, distributed derisory sums among a few of the workers and driven off with most of the proceeds. On the wall hung the obligatory portrait of Mahatma Gandhi who had warned that nationalization would make 'men moral and intellectual paupers'. Moral paupers had bankrupted the mill by buying cheap cotton at expensive prices and sharing the spoil with the merchants.

Eventually, the senior police officer managed to contact the managing director of the corporation on the phone and he agreed to talk to one of the union leaders. Although the offer made by the managing director – to do what he could to redress their grievances – seemed barely worth the cost of the call, it proved adequate to get the roadblock lifted.

Eventually, several hours late, we arrived at the rehabilitation centre where Rajnath, the young man we had been sent to see, was working. It had just been opened by the Roman Catholic diocese of Allahabad. The buildings were incomplete and there were only seven boys, all said to be former child slaves. They were being supervised by a staff of four nuns and Rajnath, whose duties seemed indeterminate.

He lined the nuns and the boys up to welcome us with flowers and oranges picked from the garden. The boys sang, danced, and raised slogans against child labour. Sanjay Ram, who was aged about ten, had been held for a year, and used to sleep outside on a roof. He looked happy and fit now, but told us he had been 'slapped and caned' if his owner was not satisfied with his work. Nandu Kumar, a big boy with a broken voice who must have been very near the minimum working age of fourteen, had been one of thirteen working for the same loom owner. Six of them had come from his home district. He didn't know where they were now.

Rajnath showed us round the new institution. Although not

particularly tall, he towered over the tiny nun who accompanied him, dressed not in the habit of her order, the Institute of the Blessed Virgin Mary, but in a green and white sari. Standing in an airy dormitory with only six double-decker bunks, he explained that the aim of the institution was to enable the boys to catch up on the school years they had lost.

Inside the institution Rajnath was clearly the boss, but once he got outside his self-confidence evaporated. He had once worked for an organization that swooped down from Delhi to raid villages where children were weaving and then beat a hasty retreat. Now that he was actually living in the carpet-weaving area, he had to be more cautious.

'You can't dial 100 and the police will come like in a big city,' he warned us. 'Anything can happen here if you're not careful. Child labour is a very delicate subject in these villages.'

He even took the precaution of taking us to meet the district magistrate before we left, so that he would be in the clear if there was any violence.

We certainly didn't get a warm welcome from the villagers of Garha. They kept their distance, until Rajnath managed to persuade them that we were journalists who had come to write about the slump in the carpet industry. One loom owner, Mumtaz Ali, was prepared to discuss that. He showed us his six looms, only three had carpets on them. Times were so bad, he said, that Obeetee was the only company which still paid advances to loom owners, and he couldn't get any work from them. Soon the villagers' curiosity got the better of them and a crowd gathered to join our discussions. Slowly, trying to hide my nervousness, I brought the subject round to child labour. This provoked an angry outburst against the NGOs who publicized the problem.

Mumtaz Ali said, 'They don't care that they are ruining our livelihood by all their bad publicity.'

Rajnath hastily assured the villagers that we were not involved in that and nor was he.

As he was speaking, a man with skeins of wool strapped to the back of his bicycle dismounted and stared at us from a distance.

Mumtaz Ali slipped away to whisper urgently to him and he hurriedly remounted his bicycle and pedalled off. When we left the village, Rajnath told us that he suspected the cyclist had some children in his weaving shed. Darkness descended and we had drawn a blank, so we agreed to return a day or two later.

On our next visit Rajnath took us to a small hamlet called Ashoknagar. We had to walk the last kilometre or so down a narrow path between two rice fields. A herd of buffaloes driven by a boy wielding a stick twice as big as he was forced us into the paddy. 'More child labour. What are you going to do about him?' I asked.

'The trouble is the poor can't wait for tomorrow. Today is what matters to them. That is the economic reality of the situation.'

The first weaving shed we came to was built of brick with a rough-and-ready thatched roof. There were four looms but only one carpet and no weavers. An elderly man dressed in a vest and dhoti followed us inside. He was introduced to me as the father of the loom owner. When asked why no one was weaving he replied, in a surly voice, 'Because all the children have gone. They've gone back to Bengal. We had to send them back.' But I did see some clothes hanging from pegs on the wall.

His son made a hurried entry, obviously worried that his father might put his foot in it. I had been told that he had been in jail for fourteen days on a charge of employing child labour, but he was adamant that he wasn't employing children now.

'It isn't worth it,' he said. 'Every contract you get says you mustn't. It's all our responsibility,' he went on bitterly. 'The companies tell us – you have to make sure there is no child labour, you have to weave the carpet right, you have to deliver the carpet on time. There is no responsibility on them, and they make all the money.'

Outside that shed we came across a young boy washing. He admitted that he was a weaver and that he came from Bengal, but he maintained that he was eighteen and there was no way of telling whether that was true or not. He certainly did not have the tiny hands that anti-slavery publicists claim are employed because they are nimble knot-tiers. Nor did the boys working for another loom owner. None of them were knotting carpets because of the Diwali holiday. They mingled quite freely with the crowd that gathered around us in the courtyard of the owner's house. There were six of them, again all from Bengal. I was assured they were over fourteen, and certainly most looked it, although I was a bit suspicious of one who was having difficulty growing his moustache. The boys themselves said they were all earning a wage and could go home whenever they wanted. 'But then,' I thought, 'they would in front of the owner.'

As we were walking back to our car, I met yet another young Bengali, Bishu, from Malda district. A cheerful young man returning from an outing to the teashop on the main road, he was not in the least shy or reticent. In spite of a mouthful of paan, he was able to tell us that he had been working as a weaver for three years, was paid according to the amount of weaving he did, and was free to come and go as he wanted. According to Bishu the loom owners go to his district and offer advances to attract weavers. There used to be younger people he said, but now they were all eighteen and above. I asked him what happened if someone who has taken an advance doesn't like the work and goes home. 'The owner says, "Bad luck. I've lost my money," I suppose,' he quipped and sauntered off.

It was obvious from our first interview that children used to be imported to work on the looms in Ashoknagar, but Rajnath said he was reasonably certain the young man was right, that there was no longer child labour there. The hamlet had been raided no less than ten times by government inspectors since January, there had also been an arrest, and so he felt the loom owners had learnt their lesson. He had no suggestions for any other village where we might expect to find children on looms.

We now needed to have a serious discussion with Edward. He invited us to breakfast in the small modern house he'd built in the compound, more convenient but less beautiful than the burra bungalow. Edward didn't want to spoil his enjoyment of a full English breakfast, and so we didn't discuss business at the table but waited until Bhagwan Das had organized the clearing away of the dishes. Then, still sitting round the table, we started.

I first reminded Edward that he had once admitted to me that he owed a debt to the foreign coverage of the carpet industry he now resented so strongly.

'Yes,' he agreed, 'until this publicity I certainly was not aware of the scale of the problem. When it was brought to our attention that made us do something. It's not a thing to be proud of but there it is. We were an out of touch management. My days of going round the looms had ended many years previously.'

'So why do you feel so strongly about the anti-child labour campaign now?'

'Because they exaggerate, and they are in the hands of NGOs like Rugmark whose business it is to paint as bleak a picture as possible. If they don't, who will support them?'

I knew that Edward's company now took stringent measures to try to ensure that no children were employed on their looms and so I couldn't really understand why Edward refused to cooperate with Rugmark.

But he explained, 'I find their methods and claims unacceptable. And don't think we haven't paid a price, we have, we have suffered because of the propaganda organized by Rugmark.'

We were joined by Vinoo Sharma, a member of an old Mirzapur family who had spent his whole career working with Edward in Obeetee. Edward had wisely left most of the negotiations with Rugmark to Vinoo, who was less excitable and more diplomatic. He explained that Obeetee had been involved in the original negotiations which led to the formation of Rugmark. The negotiations had broken down because Vinoo had argued that inspection of carpet looms had to be done professionally. It couldn't be done by an NGO. He had even suggested two professional companies. One had refused to even consider inspecting such a complicated industry. Vinoo showed us a letter from the other company, SGS India Ltd, the branch of a Swiss company, which did send representatives to Mirzapur. On their return the company wrote, 'It will not be feasible to monitor on a regular basis to ensure that carpets woven at various and far-flung units are meeting the required criteria.'

One of the phrases that always crops up in anti-child slavery campaigns is 'India has the largest number of child labourers', a phrase which ignores the fact that India probably has the largest number of children in the world. China is the only other country which might just have more, and that is unlikely if the claims made for its family planning programme are valid. What is more, there is very little information about child labour in China because the authorities don't exactly welcome investigations into such matters.

When I put those points to Edward he exploded. 'Why do they always target India? I'll tell you why. Because they can get away with it here; it's a soft target because it's an open country. They have no wish apparently to disturb the ayatollahs and they don't wish to join with the victims of Tiananmen Square, so Chinese and Iranian carpets are exempted.'

A video of the Channel 4 film *Slavery*, with the most recent Rugmark publicity, had just arrived in Mirzapur. I suggested that Edward should watch it with us, but that was a mistake.

'I can't bear to see all that exaggeration,' he said. 'It makes me sick.'

We left Edward and set off for the burra bungalow. Edward's golden labrador Tipu, out for his morning walk, bounded towards us. Butterflies, pale blue, black and white with red spots, brown, and peacock-eyed orange, fluttered about lantana bushes. Banana plants were so heavily laden with fruit they had to be held up by stout bamboos. There were dark green-leafed mango trees as well as jackfruit, orange and grapefruit trees. In the distance we could see an extensive vegetable garden. Neat red gravel paths edged by upturned bricks criss-crossed the compound.

We passed under three horseshoes above the door of the bungalow, not a common sight in India where a tulsi bush is the customary auspicious symbol, and took our seats to watch the video with the heads of the last leopards to be shot by the Oakley family before hunting was banned staring down at us.

The section of the television programme which dealt with India was the story of a child slave called Huru and his rescue. He had been located and rescued by volunteers from the South Asian Coalition on Child Servitude, a Delhi-based organization which is

the main Indian NGO supporter of Rugmark. The script maintained that as many as 300,000 children were enslaved on India's
carpet looms. It suggested SACCS was the only organization
looking for child slaves and, as part of the promotion of Rugmark,
estimated that 'as many as nine out of ten carpets which don't carry
the Rugmark label may have been touched by the small hands of
slavery'. This, if true, would inevitably mean that some of the
biggest carpet manufacturers who were not supporting the scheme
were regularly exporting carpets woven by children. We saw the
scene which had enraged Robin Garland – Dr Alan Knight,
the ethical trading director of B&Q, standing in front of a pile
of the cheapest carpets, promoting Rugmark and suggesting that
other carpets might well have been woven by 'a ten-year-old slave
in India strapped to his loom making this rug for twenty hours a
day'.

Vinoo muttered, 'That's nonsense. Weaving a rug requires con-
centration and no child could weave for twenty hours a day without
producing a botched job which would be rejected by the manufacturer.'

Dr Alan Knight was no fool. When I spoke to him about this
film he pointed out that Rugmark had the backing of Christian
Aid, Oxfam, and other British NGOs. He saw the label as an answer
to the dilemma buyers face when they are expected to find solutions to the ethical issues in the supply chains they buy from. The
only other practical way for B&Q to handle the pressure from
NGOs would be not to buy Indian carpets, 'and who would that
help?' Dr Knight asked me. But he had been put in a false position,
led into making an exaggerated claim by overstated campaigns
against child labour.

During the scene when the raid took place, Vinoo became even
more suspicious. The police seemed remarkably inactive, there was
no sign of the senior official of the government who ought to have
been there, and the name of the village was not mentioned. 'I
wouldn't necessarily say that's a put-up job,' he said, 'but it certainly
doesn't seem to be the official raid they claim.'

Vinoo pointed out other strange circumstances in the film. The father had asked SACCS to find his child, but did not have the first idea where the boy was. So how had SACCS located him? If there really were 300,000 slave children spread over thousands of square miles, it would mean they had found a needle in a haystack. The journalists posed as carpet buyers to meet the loom owner, who didn't actually turn up, but sent his representative along. According to Vinoo, importers would not normally deal with a loom owner but with the next step up the ladder, the manufacturer who com- missioned the loom owner.

We had already heard of a raid which had been filmed a few months ago in a village near Mirzapur. The district magistrate told us he had no knowledge of that raid, and so we thought perhaps that was the Channel 4 raid and it had been staged by SACCS. But then we found two representatives of the Bachpan Bachao Andolan, the member of the SACCS coalition that conducts raids in the carpet belt. They were hanging around a shop which sold marble. Apparently the proprietor, Rama Shankar Chaurasia, was the general secretary of SACCS. He was away in Delhi where he spent most of his time. His shops – he also owned one which hired out tents for weddings and other functions – as well as the raids were looked after by his son, Rajesh. He was somewhere else in the town 'on business' we were told by a young man wearing a scruffy baseball cap on his shaven head.

'You can speak to me. I am authorized, I'm district coordinator,' Sudhir Varma said, revealing paan-stained teeth. Pointing to another young man leaning against the counter of the shop he went on, 'This is my colleague Dinesh Yadav. He is a volunteer.'

Although of a more humble status, Dinesh Yadav – a self-confident or perhaps I should say cocksure young man – took over as the spokesman. He maintained that the movement made a lot of raids, six, seven or ten a month, sometimes two or three in a day. This year they had released 165 slave children. When we asked for details of the raids in Mirzapur district, Dinesh became a little less confident, 'There were some bonded adults released, I think, on the 3rd of January and some children on the 6th or 7th of January.'

It was by now the end of October.

The coordinator came to his rescue, 'We will have to look at the files and we can't do that because Rajeshji is not here.'

They seemed a little too surprised when asked about the raid which had been filmed near Mirzapur recently. They knew nothing, but nothing, about that, but when we asked about the Channel 4 filming, Dinesh was able to give us the precise location and date – village Vishwanathpur on 28 December 1999.

Although SACCS is closely associated with Rugmark, Dinesh maintained he had found children working on looms which were licensed by the foundation. 'Half their looms are not registered and they check only the registered ones,' he said scornfully.

Pushing his cap to the back of his head, Sudhir sneered, 'The exporters make fools of the Rugmark people. They will write that they are using one loom, and take work from another.'

We asked Sudhir whether he had ever found children on the looms of Obeetee or Hill and Company. Without any sign of reluctance, which surprised us because we knew how bad the relationship between SACCS and Obeetee was, he said, 'Obeetee and Hill don't have child labour. They have their own inspectors.'

That was a claim Edward himself would never make. He would only say that Obeetee did their best to ensure there was no child labour on their looms.

One mystery about the Channel 4 film remained to be cleared up – how had SACCS found a specific child when his father did not have the first idea where he was? I asked Dinesh how they located children.

'Mainly we know the child's address, the child sends a letter home, or there are labourers all from the same village, and one goes home.'

Sudhir interrupted hurriedly, 'Doesn't go home, you mean to say escapes.'

'But,' I insisted, 'supposing you don't have an address at all, how do you find a boy you have been asked to locate?'

'That's a huge problem. We can't do that,' Dinesh admitted.

Just to be absolutely sure about the Channel 4 raid, we drove the next day to Gyanpur where the sub-divisional magistrate – who, we were told, had accompanied the SACCS volunteers – was posted. He had been transferred, as is the way of things in Uttar Pradesh. But we did manage to find a more junior revenue official, naib tehsildar Ganpat Ram, sitting outside the yellow concrete box the government had allocated to him as his quarters in the compound, which separated the administration from the people of Gyanpur. A defunct hand-pump stood in a puddle of stagnant water surrounded by weeds. Here, apparently, the administrators of Uttar Pradesh didn't even seem able to look after themselves. The naib tehsildar was relaxing in a vest and lungi before going to work. When we asked him about the Channel 4 raid he said, 'This raid did take place. It was official because the magistrate gave permission and the labour officer and naib tehsildar went along with them.'

There is an unpleasant side to journalism, and to all journalists, and I have to admit to feeling disappointed that the naib tehsildar had spoilt a 'good story'. Good in that context nearly always means bad for someone else, and it would have been bad news for Channel 4 if there had been no official record of the raid. But that would have only been an incidental bonus. We had not come to Mirzapur to investigate the film, but to tell the story of Edward Oakley and his battle with Rugmark, to discover whether this was another case of a misconceived First World intervention in a Third World problem, or an obstinate expatriate businessman refusing to collaborate in an effective scheme to prevent child labour and save the carpet industry. To tell that story fully we had to see what steps Obeetee were taking to prevent children weaving their carpets.

The factory where the wool is dyed before it's distributed to the weavers, and where the carpets are finished when they come off the loom, is in the town of Gopiganj across the Ganges from the company headquarters. The factory is ancient and modern. Old-fashioned balances, instead of modern scales, weigh wool in the yarn shed. Stokers streaked with coal dust labour to keep a boiler in steam. A brass plate on the boiler reads: Engineers Yates and Thorn, 1921, Blackburn. But just beyond the boiler is a modern plant for treating effluent, and in the office is an air-conditioned room with a battery of computer screens. This is where the records of looms are kept.

Mithilesh Kumar, the dapper senior vice-president accompanying us, punched in a number and on the screen appeared a buyer's code, an order number, a design code, a loom owner's name, details of the progress on a carpet, and a depot code. Obeetee apparently has twenty-five depots spread over fourteen districts. Each depot has loom supervisors and inspectors whose job it is to ensure that no children are weaving Obeetee carpets. Mithilesh Kumar gave the computer another order, and up came more details of the loom owner including the names of every member of the family. This meant that if any children were discovered on the loom, Obeetee would know whether they belonged to the owner's family or not.

Mithilesh Kumar admitted that Obeetee inspectors did sometimes find children, and that was why the company could not give an absolute guarantee.

'It's very rare now, however,' he said. 'People know that Obeetee polices their looms and if they find children the company people rush to the spot, verify, remove the loom owner's card, and they lose work.'

Just down the road from Obeetee's factory was Rugmark's office, from which they monitored 28,000 looms working for 225 exporters. They did not have offices or officials spread throughout the areas where their registered looms were located, although they had to carry out inspections in twenty-nine districts, many more than Obeetee's fourteen. Rugmark's eleven inspectors were based in Gopiganj itself, or in Varanasi. They had a computer, but the day we called on them unexpectedly, the only person who could operate it was on leave. The office itself was on the ground floor of a large house and Rashid Raza, the coordinator of inspection and monitoring, told us the computer was often out of action because the electricity supply was erratic and the landlord wouldn't let them use a noisy generator. The recent records all seemed to have been handwritten.

Rashid Raza was a youngish man who obviously sincerely believed that Rugmark's claims were valid.

'Ninety-nine per cent we can guarantee that no child has worked on a carpet,' he said. 'And I can give a total guarantee that if a child is working he will be caught.'

But he did admit there was a problem with exporters who did not declare all the looms on which their carpets were being woven. The problem was compounded by exporters' reluctance to provide up-to-date lists of their looms. He told us, 'Some unlisted looms we do find, some we don't. The difficulty is that most exporters do not know where their goods are being woven.'

Recent economies had lowered the inspectors' effectiveness. They used to travel by car but now went out in pairs on motorcycles, which had reduced their range and meant the loom inspections were almost entirely concentrated within two circles each with a radius of fifty kilometres from Varanasi or Gopiganj, circles which must have overlapped.

'There is a problem,' Rashid agreed, 'but there are advantages. A car can't go into the interior and people can see in advance a car is coming, with a motorcycle people's suspicions are not aroused.'

Rashid broke off the conversation to take a telephone call from another room. He returned looking very pleased, sat down, and said with a satisfied smile, 'Well you are in luck, one of our teams has found a child labourer.'

We couldn't go straight to the loom because Rashid didn't know its location, and so we had to drive to the home of one of the inspectors and wait for him to return. His house was in the shadow of the tall brick-built chimney of Hill and Company's factory. Some of the company's work was contracted out to people living around the factory. In one house down the road from where the inspector lived artists were colouring maps of carpets and in another I saw a sight I had not seen on the earlier visit to Mirzapur and its surroundings. A young man was hammering what looked like a chisel into a carpet stretched so taut that the weaving appeared to have been pulled apart. Rashid explained that with each tap on the chisel the craftsman moved one knot to straighten what I could see was a very crooked line. As he moved the knots a gap opened up which would apparently close when the carpet was released from its stranglehold. The tool the craftsman was using turned out to have the head of a chisel but with a very fine point, like a needle. Nevertheless, anyone who didn't have the excellent eyesight, the steady hand, and the coordination of the craftsman, would do severe damage to any carpet with that implement.

As we walked on and the tapping of the hammer died away, I said to Rashid, 'The poor guy who wove that carpet must have paid a heavy price for making such a mess of it.'

Eventually the two inspectors returned from their day's work. It turned out that they had not found one, but two looms with children on them. They showed us the inspection reports. On loom listed number 52, in Jigna village, some forty kilometres from Mirzapur, a child had been found weaving a carpet for a listed manufacturer, Madhu Carpets. It was a sad case. The boy's father was handicapped and his elder brother, who was working on the loom beside him, only had one leg. The inspectors said the child labourer himself was about thirteen.

The other child had been working in Mirzapur itself, and so we decided to go to see that loom. As we approached the garage of a house in the centre of the town, we heard what sounded like the clicking of a battery of knitting needles. When we got there, we saw nine young men sitting in front of metal looms jabbing needles into the threads of the wefts. They were mechanical needles which clicked each time they injected and cut a tuft of wool. None of the weavers of these tufted carpets, very much cheaper than the hand-knotted variety, was under age, but standing in one corner, silent and confused, was a boy wearing trousers and a vest, yellow with age, which revealed the ribs sticking out from his chest.

The looms were being supervised by the owner's brother. As soon as he saw the inspectors he started to protest, 'It's not our fault that this boy was working. His father begged us to give him a job because he needed the money.'

Rashid Raza reassured him, 'I am not here to get you arrested. I am here to find out what should be done.'

But he continued to argue, 'The exporter's name on your forms them. The only difference is that we come under the discipline of the Archbishop of Goa, while the Jesuits and others have a direct line to Rome; they bypass the archbishop.'

Very sure of his vocation, which he had tried sorely by living for twelve years in a hut among some of the poorest people in India, Father Sebi agreed with the Jesuit from Bom Jesus that, in spite of all its efforts, the Inquisition was never able to eradicate the Hindu influence on Goan Christianity. When he was working among the tribals of Nagar Haveli, north of Goa on the western coast, Father Sebi would always celebrate mass sitting cross-legged on the floor with the villagers. He didn't wear a cassock or any vestments, only a shawl round his shoulders. Mind you, none of the Pilar fathers seemed to wear their cassocks very often. Father Sebi himself was sporting a very bright pink, white and blue bush shirt.

'We have to accept that our people and, indeed, we clergy too have very Hindu hearts,' he explained. 'In Goa there are so many crosses and saints everywhere. You must have seen them. But what do the saints mean? When we were converted we all had a family god and we found it easy to replace them with Saint Antony or someone like that, so in some ways devotion to saints has its roots in Hinduism. It is Latin influence but very Indian.'

Some Goan Catholics still also worshipped in temples. Father Sebi told us a story of a priest who had gone to a temple dressed in kurta and pajamas to look like a Hindu. He and some friends watched the devotees going in with their gifts for the deity and coming out again with *tikas* on their foreheads. Eventually they saw a father and son who were wearing crosses round their necks. The priest adopted a Hindu accent – there is a difference in the way that Hindus and Christians speak in Goa – and said how pleased he was that Christians felt welcome in the temple, but then asked, 'Does the Christian religion allow you to worship a Hindu God?' The Christian replied nervously, 'Our priests shouldn't know we've been here.' The priest put them at ease: 'Don't worry, we won't tell anyone. We understand you because we Hindus also like to go to Christian churches, but you are allowed to take our prasad and you won't let us take yours.' That did shock the Christians. 'Ours is the body and blood of Christ, it would be a sin for you to take it. Even we can't take it if we've sinned.'

When the priest asked, 'Have you sinned by coming to the temple?' it was too much for the Christian. He took his son's hand and walked away.

Father Sebi had seen the state of Western Christendom when he was sent to Germany for further studies in theology. He knew all about the shortage of priests and perhaps secretly rejoiced (although he never said as much) in the opportunity the Pilar fathers now had to reverse history by sending missionaries to Europe and America. He told us with some pride that Pilar fathers had taken over the parish of Deptford in south London.

'That's a remarkable turn round,' I said, 'but why isn't the church on the decline here? How is it that your mass-attendances are keeping up as well as all those vocations?'

Father Sebi rubbed his black-bearded chin and thought before answering, 'Well, I don't know whether I should go on about our Hindu hearts, but at least I can say that, for all the Western trappings you see in the church here, and those centuries of Portuguese influence, we remain oriental. There isn't that Western separation of God and us humans, God is in a sense within us. Here also it's taken for granted that you believe in God, it's not like in the West, you don't question. God belongs to your life, God is in you.'

After lunch in the refectory of crispy Goan-style fried fish, fish and vegetable curries too, and plenty of rice – far less spartan than I'd feared – we went to the top of the seminary to see the chapel.

It was a plain rectangular room, with a dome over the marble altar and stained glass windows in the far wall. Father Sebi pointed to the depiction of the Virgin Mary in one of the windows and said, 'We wanted Mary to be wearing a sari, but when the windows came back from the stained-glass makers in Cologne, she was in the robes of a Western Mother of God. That's the problem. We want to acknowledge the Indian in our church, but the West won't go away. Next week the Pilar fathers will be celebrating a public mass on Indian independence day, and it will include Hindu rituals like *aarti* and smearing *kumkum* on the forehead. Our people will take that provided it's just once in a while, but basically, Christians here outwardly still want to be Westernized. We must become an Indian church, and we must be seen to become one, otherwise the rest of the country will not accept us, but we mustn't go too fast or else the passengers will get off the bus.'

There is one Indian tradition, though, that the Goan church of today does want to eliminate – caste. Throughout more than four hundred years of missionary activity, the church, sometimes reluctantly sometimes less so, accepted caste divisions in Indian Christianity. The seventeenth-century Jesuit Robert de Nobili, who is reputed to have converted some 100,000 south Indians, advised missionaries 'to see which of the customs of the place is not sinful and can be used to further God's religion. After having decided then he must follow those customs himself.' Having judged that caste was not sinful, de Nobili set about living like a Brahmin himself, because he believed this was the only way to convert them. He even avoided any contacts with castes the Brahmins regarded as impure. De Nobili was summoned to Goa to explain himself, but in the end it was decided that he could continue living as a Brahmin.

Pope Alexander II was concerned about the impact of caste on the clergy. In 1658 he decreed, 'The schools should be open to all, although to avoid fighting the low-caste children should be separated from the rest. But those of the low caste and the ignorant should on no account be excluded from holy communion. The sick should be visited and the viaticum should be taken to them no matter how miserable be their huts.' In the nineteenth century, Pope Benedict XIV had to make it clear that high- and low-caste Christians should hear mass in the same church at the same time. The Jesuit missionaries of that century were divided, with the French believing that caste divisions should be accepted, the Irish opposing them, and the Italians being split on the issue.

In Portuguese Goa the church lived with caste. The higher castes were members of the confrarias, or committees, which controlled the village churches. They sat in the front pews at mass, and they organized and played the prominent roles in annual festivals. Upper-caste families had a tradition of sending one son into the church so that they dominated the diocesan clergy too. In democratic India the lower-caste Christians became assertive and the hierarchy came under pressure to ensure that there were no longer any second-class citizens of the kingdom of God here on earth.

In the rector's hall of the Diocesan Seminary, which stands on a hillock that was once the site of an important fortress, a massive white building, looking not entirely unmilitary itself, we were told of a recent caste crisis in the church. The rector of the seminary, whose name we could barely believe was Father Tommas d'Aquino, said he'd had to agree to his professor of moral theology taking charge of the parish of Cuncolim because no other priest was willing to go there after a dispute over membership of the committee which controlled the church properties. The lower castes had insisted that the upper castes' monopoly of the committee should be broken. They had also demanded a role in the patronal festival and, when this had been refused, they had boycotted the village celebrations and gone to a shrine near Panaji to commemorate their patron saint. But Father Tommas was confident the upper castes had now learnt their lesson. 'They are frightened,' he said, 'because the whole voice of the church has been raised.'

Father Tommas was under fifty, younger than I had expected, the rector of the seminary to be, and seemed very anxious to convince us that he was no narrow-minded traditionalist, but he did tell us with some pride that he came from a traditional family, which I assumed meant upper caste. 'My generation arrived with some baggage from home,' he said, 'respect for elders, home education, and all that. Now we get seminarians from the rural areas and from families which never had priests before and they don't have that baggage.'

He also seemed to regret what he saw as a lack of rigour in the seminary. In his days as a seminarian, teachers had been venerable figures, awe inspiring, like the portraits of past archbishops, and indeed the present one, staring severely from the walls of the bleak hall. Now, according to the rector all the students were 'his pals'. I couldn't quite square this with his admission that last year the drop-out rate was thirty-five per cent which included several seminarians expelled for 'intellectual or moral deficiency'. But Father Tommas maintained that was exceptional.

When pressed on the quality of the vocations, Father Tommas said, 'They are different, they are not what they used to be, but that's good because they don't carry the same subculture with them.' Decoded, that meant they came from the lower castes. I could not help wondering whether Father Tommas really felt that was good.

A friend living in the nearby village of Loutulim had suggested that after the seminary we should call on his parish priest, a man who didn't carry the same baggage as the rector. Our taxi driver had the greatest difficulty in picking his way through the puddled potholes, fast being turned into floods by the monsoon rains. His task was not helped by his only wiper's inability to cope with the waterfall flowing down the windscreen, but we did eventually reach the clergy house of Loutulim, which was as usual built on to the church. We made our way up a path, the rain beating down on our umbrellas, and found a servant, or he may have been the verger, waiting for us at the door. We followed him along a dark, dank passage, and up a dimly lit flight of well-trodden stairs. The house was more like an institution than a home, an institution that was distinctly down at heel, and very short on inmates, but the parish priest, Father Joseph Cajetan d'Costa, had managed to make the one room he lived in bright and cheerful. Although he was off-duty, watching television with a friend, he welcomed us intruders warmly.

This was our first meeting with a parish priest, one of the foot soldiers of the church. Father d'Costa must have been in his forties but, although his hair had turned grey in the service of the church, he still had a young, unlined face, and did not seem to be oppressed by any of the cares that weigh heavily on clergy in the Western church – loneliness, lack of response, doubt and depression – living, as they do, in a world where Mammon is triumphant and God on the retreat. In Loutulim half the eight thousand parishioners still come to mass every Sunday. Father d'Costa confirmed that he did not come from one of those high-caste families who had once dominated the church – his father was a farmer in a predominantly

Hindu village that had never produced a priest before. This had caused some problems in his earlier parishes.

'The influential people did not always show me proper respect,' Father d'Costa admitted. 'They didn't like it when I opposed their selfish interests. They wanted to grab church properties and if you didn't let them they talked against you. And they gave privileges undue importance, and if you didn't give them, then they turned against you.'

'What do you mean by privileges?' I asked.

'Brahmins, you know, they think themselves superior. They want all privileges for themselves. For instance they say only they can carry the cross on Good Friday. This they maintain has always been their tradition and should remain so.'

'So did this discourage you, make you wonder about a church which has upheld such unfair, unChristian privileges?'

'No, I felt happy to suffer for a good cause, to identify with Christ through suffering.'

'What about this parish, has it been easier here?'

Father d'Costa replied hurriedly, as if anxious to reassure me, 'No, no, there are no disruptive elements here, here people are cooperative and loving.' He paused before adding, 'But I am of course new here,' and for the first time he looked crestfallen. It was clear he feared there might be more suffering ahead.

The narrow road back from Loutulim to Panaji runs along the southern bank of the mouth of the River Zuari. On the day we travelled, there seemed to be an inordinate amount of heavy vehicles on what was a comparatively minor road. Our driver explained that the traffic had been diverted because the bridge on the main north–south road was in urgent need of repair and had been closed to heavy vehicles. When the Portuguese left Goa, there were no bridges over the Zuari or over the Mandovi. The capital Panaji was still effectively an island. Even when the Indian administration did build a bridge over the Mandovi it collapsed after a few years, and had to be rebuilt. Now the Zuari bridge appeared to be in danger of suffering the same fate. Inevitably, the shortcomings in the construction of the bridges were attributed to corruption with the connivance of politicians – contractors paying bribes so that substandard material and short cuts went officially unnoticed. The church in Goa, which had once lent on the state for support, now felt so self-confident that it was not afraid to oppose the government, especially on this issue of corruption. But corruption wasn't the first issue which brought the church into politics.

After 'liberation', Goan Christians feared their tiny enclave would be submerged in the vast ocean of India. That fear became very real with the formation of a party which was overtly Hindu, and determined to merge Goa with its neighbour to the north, the vast state of Maharashtra, and its capital Bombay, that was more than twelve hours away by road and twenty-two by sea. The Maharashtra Gomantak Party wanted to destroy Goa's separate identity in order to undermine the church's influence and to diminish the value of the Christian vote, which was approximately thirty-two per cent in Goa but would have been a drop in the ocean of Maharashtra. It aimed to ensure that government perks and privileges, especially jobs, now went to Hindus. Although the position of the church was delicate, it took the risk and plunged into politics to fight for Goa's separate existence.

Wherever we went we were told, 'You should go and see Willy if you want to know about the church and politics.' Willy, or Dr Wilfred de Souza, is also known as 'double FRCS' because he returned home in 1962 after passing the exams set by the Royal College of Surgeons in London, and appearing successfully before the surgeons of Edinburgh too. When he returned to Goa he found there was no other surgeon and so, with the double FRCS to boost his reputation, he soon found plenty of work. His bungalow, set in a well-tended garden, was in a village to the north of Panaji. He'd not only brought an English wife back with him from his days in training but also a passion for dogs. His dachshund was the largest Gilly or I had ever seen, and there was a friendly Labrador, and a spaniel too.

Willy himself was a small, round, white-haired Pickwickian figure. He was wearing the uniform of a successful doctor, shining white trousers and an equally white bush shirt. I asked why, after spending all those years in training and passing such difficult exams, he'd deserted medicine for politics.

'I was dragged into politics,' he said, leaning back in his elaborately carved Goan baroque chair. 'It was a matter of life and death, we had to defend our identity. But I never gave up medicine. I was operating even when I was Chief Minister.'

'Was Christianity under threat?' I asked.

'Well, I wouldn't go as far as that,' replied Dr Willy, 'but the church felt it necessary to play a big role. Basically the lower standard of Christians was influenced by the church.'

'What do you mean by lower standard?'

Dr Willy was embarrassed. 'Well, you know, the less well educated, the less well off.'

'The lower caste?'

As a good politician he didn't answer that one but went on, 'The priests, who usually guide lay people, were all against the merger. They supported our United Goan Party because it was a Christian party.'

'But wasn't that bringing politics into religion?' I asked.

Dr Willy wasn't having any of that. 'They were playing very dirty,' he shot back. 'A very prominent politician from Maharashtra came here and called Christians "black Portuguese". When people use tactics like that, what do you expect us to do, lie down and be trodden all over?'

In the end it was a division in the Hindu community that saved the day for Goa. The Maharashtrian party had become so closely identified with the lower castes, that the upper-caste Hindus voted against them when a referendum on the merger was held, and Goa retained its separate identity.

Two more issues had to be fought before Dr Willy was satisfied. The merger had been defeated but that didn't mean Goa could administer itself, it was still controlled by the central government in Delhi. Dr Willy believed Goa would not be safe until it became a fully-fledged state of the Indian Union governed by its own assembly. Then there was the question of the state language. The Maharashtrian lobby wanted their language Marathi, while the language of Christians, and indeed of many Hindus, was Goa's own Konkani.

Dr Willy sought the help of the church to fight those battles too, and once again together they won. An independent state did come into existence with Konkani as its official language. The language decision was not as clear cut as the church would have liked, as it also allowed Marathi to be used for official business. The church, in its Pastoral Review, described the compromise as bigamy, but decided to live with this sin.

That, according to Dr Willy, was the end of the church's involvement in politics. 'The church doesn't take part in the political scene any more,' he said in such a determined manner it appeared he'd ordered it to clear off his political patch. 'In fact religion should be removed from politics altogether. I am a Catholic in so far as I go to church on Sundays and say my prayers, but I am not a Catholic politician.'

I didn't care to remind Dr Willy that he was once a Catholic politician by his own admission, fighting alongside the church, and it was his politics which helped the church get over its Portuguese hangover. Just when it needed a new identity, it was given the opportunity to do battle as a defender of Goan culture. Because the church needed the support of the Hindu elite it didn't fall into the trap of presenting that culture as Christian. So from being a colonial church it became a church of what I suppose one would call Goan sub-nationalism. To have claimed to be nationalist would have offended the Indian government, and the church was too astute to do that.

Not all politicians agree with Dr Willy that the church is no longer involved in politics, nor indeed do all priests. Father José Dias, for instance, the priest of a parish a few miles down the road from Dr Willy's village is renowned for his political activities. Although his church, St Alex Calangute, was built by Franciscans, whom historians of Goan architecture have described as more sober in their habits than some of the other church-building orders, it nevertheless has ornate towers on both sides of the façade and between them is a dome with a turret and a cross on top of it.

Flanked by palm trees, the church used to stand on its own, an imposing white landmark dominating the flat countryside, but now a line of identical apartments painted a hideous pink which clashes with the emerald-green paddy fields, stands just the other side of the road, destroying St Alex's isolation. No attempt, either architectural or horticultural, has been made to disguise this scar on the landscape.

When we met Father José in his house, which was also built on to the church, he was wearing his white cassock because he hadn't had time to change after celebrating mass at six o'clock in the morning. It was by now nearly midday and a young couple were still waiting outside his room to discuss arrangements for their wedding. Although Father José is renowned for his involvement in environmental issues – he had been arrested three times during the protest movement which failed to prevent the government building a railway line across coastal Goa – he was still first and foremost a priest. 'I've been ordained for twenty years and I'm very happy with my ministry,' he told us speaking fast and earnestly. 'I feel I have a vocation, and I am quite clear about my identity. Those priests who have problems do so because they have identity crises.'

Slight, with gold-rimmed glasses, Father José seemed the last person you'd expect to come from a family in such a robust profession as the merchant navy, but his home was St Stephen's island in the Mandovi river renowned for its 'shippies'. His father and all his brothers sailed with P&O. When I asked whether as officers or men he replied very firmly, 'Men.'

He is one of those priests who have taken up what is known in the church as 'the option for the poor'. In Goa, as elsewhere in the world, that is a political option, and although many of the issues he has been involved in are environmental, they also involve politics and economics. Father José's own parish was little more than a fishing village thirty years ago, but then the hippy movement discovered the seven kilometres of Calangute beach. The hippies paved the way for both package tours and five-star tourism. Now behind the beach stands a jumble of hotels, hostels, and holiday homes, restaurants and bars, shacks, stalls, and shops. To add to the

ugliness, this monsoon the rough seas had washed a sizeable freighter
on to the beach. No one seemed to know what to do with it. The
manager of the five-star resort whose beach the ship was parked
on said he'd protested but nothing had happened. He could only
hope that something would happen before the start of the tourist
season.

Father José was currently campaigning against the corruption
which has made a mockery of every effort to control the development of Calangute. He showed us an article in the latest edition of
his parish magazine blaming the greed and corruption of his own
parishioners. The writer complained, 'We, the people of Calangute,
are now ever willing to buy favours. We want the authorities to
legalize our irregularities and regularize our irregularities. We want
to cut a tree without permission, build our houses in violation of
zoning and building laws, construct an illegal hotel and block
people's access to some villagers' traditional pathway, pay the public
health officer to look the other way, produce false certificates, alter
land records.'

Father José laughed when I told him that Dr Willy described one
former chief minister as the second St Francis Xavier because he
was so successful at converting – converting agricultural land into
land for building construction.

The parish priest was also involved in attempting to prevent a
company called Meta Strips manufacturing brass strips from the
copper in disused cables. Copper is officially classed as hazardous
waste and 70 per cent of the imported cables would have been
coated with PVC, a plastic notoriously difficult to dispose of.
Furthermore, the process of converting copper into brass would
have required vast amounts of fresh water, a resource that Goa was
chronically short of.

Father José was very anxious to impress on us that this was 'a
people's campaign' involving Goans of all religions. 'We didn't want
the church to give the lead,' he said. 'We only wanted, and we got,
its support.' But the church had still played a very prominent role,
so much so that it's been the target of an apparently orchestrated campaign of legal threats. The church's spokesman had received a series

of nearly identical lawyers' letters from aggrieved shareholders, claiming that the campaign against Meta Strips had prevented the factory starting production and thus robbed them of their dividend. The letters accused the church of 'misguiding the innocent, poor and illiterate people of the villages surrounding the factory and inciting and abetting them to indulge in large-scale unlawful agitation against the factory by resorting to violent means'. The church was also charged with 'arm-twisting' the government to order an 'illegal' closure of the factory. The shareholders all threatened legal action unless the church paid substantial sums of money in compensation.

There have been efforts to turn the public against the church by accusing it of communal politics – of mixing religion with politics. That failed because, as Father José explained, 'We had earlier opposed a nylon plant which businessmen wanted to put up in a Hindu area of the state, and so we had already demonstrated that we were not interested in environmental issues for communal reasons. There never was a communal issue in Goa, and still is only when politicians manipulate it.'

Father José maintains that political corruption is at the root of all the issues he has been involved in. 'These projects,' he explained, 'are taken up by the rich against the poor. The poor elect the politicians, but once elected they don't care for the poor, only for the multimillionaires and multinationals who can pay them for their services. If they didn't pay the politicians would have no interest in bending the environment laws, and all the laws in fact.'

Father José took notes of what he was saying when he got excited. Attacking a plan to build a new airport, which he maintained was quite unnecessary, he spelt out verbally and on paper, 'Four thousand crores, ten per cent commission – four hundred crores.'

He went on to say, 'Politicians are no better than the British or the Portuguese colonialists – they only differed in colour. We are now waiting for the second liberation, and I am not very keen on celebrating the first one.'

That was fighting talk in a state where it's not always wise to cast doubt on your loyalty to India. But Father José is not a lone voice in the church. When we went to call on the spokesman of the archdiocese of Goa, to get the official view about the church and politics, he said, 'It is our Christian duty to attack political corruption. In our sermons we preach about corruption. Nothing is done, everything is delayed because the politicians and officials wait for bribes.'

Surprised that the official spokesman for a traditionally conservative organization, whose relations with the government were always delicate, should be so outspoken, I asked, 'Are you sure you want to be quoted on that?'

'Why not? The politicians themselves admit there is corruption everywhere.'

The spokesman then produced a book by Luizinho Falero, a former chief minister of Goa, and showed me that he'd written, 'Corruption breeds corruption and it is a price tag the citizen is willing to pay and the politician is eager to take.'

The church would not have remained a powerful political force in Goa, able to challenge corrupt politicians, bureaucrats, and businessmen, the nexus which holds India in thrall, if it hadn't retained the loyalty of its own people. Fortunately, just at the time the church in Goa needed to change if it was not to be identified with an era that had passed, the Second Vatican Council forced change on it. A priest-ridden, authoritative church, with a clergy educated in a foreign tongue, a Latin liturgy and mystical rituals, was told by the Council that it had to involve the laity. So the priest celebrating mass moved down from the distant, dark, high altar where he was dwarfed by the Portuguese baroque reredos, to the chancel steps. The preacher moved out of the ornate pulpit set in one of the walls of the nave, high above the congregation, and spoke from the floor of the church. The laity took on the readings from the Old Testament and the Epistles. The priest who had been set apart as the representative of a majestic God, became one with his parishioners worshipping a personal God, more a friend than a king.

Not all the changes came as rapidly as they should and some have still not been completed. Although the liturgy was now celebrated in Konkani, the translation of the New Testament was not finished until 1973 and there was still work to be done on the Old Testament. The changes that were made did not go far enough for some. In the 1970s Catholics started deserting the church for charismatic sects. 'Believers' as they are known in Goa.

On the outskirts of the town of Margao there is a Coca-Cola bottling plant and right next to it a new red-brick building which looks not unlike a Swiss chalet. It's the headquarters of the Good News Church. Ranjeet Rodrigues, the young leader of the church and his assistant, Sharmila de Souza, had both been Roman Catholics and confirmed that most of their members had come from the church too. The leader said, 'They come for the message that Jesus forgives sin. I was a Roman Catholic, I kept all their rules and rituals, but there was nothing there to deal with my knowledge that I was a sinner. It didn't touch my life.'

'Did you speak to a priest before leaving the church?' I asked.

'Yes, I told priests that penance was not a Bible concept, that nowhere in the Bible did it talk of the structure of the church, and so many other things they were doing were not biblical. They tried to dissuade me, but all they could say was, "That's the way it's been for the last five hundred years and that's the way it will always be," which doesn't satisfy anyone.'

The Roman Catholic church did some research of its own on why people were leaving to become Believers. Eighty per cent said it was for 'the God experience'. Their second reason was 'the primacy given to the word of God'. The third was 'fellowship and personalized pastoral care'. To combat this, in 1974 the church imported the Catholic charismatic movement which had started in America.

We were told there was a Catholic charismatic service every Friday in the parish church of Mandur. The Friday we chose to go there the monsoon was in spate again and we wondered whether our journey would be in vain, whether the service would be washed out. But when we lost our way in the narrow country lanes and asked directions from a somewhat bedraggled man who, it turned out, had just come from the service, he was able to assure us there was a full congregation, and several hours still to go. Following his directions we came to a village green on which the white church of Our Lady of Refuge stood. Rows of cars and scooters were parked outside and the church was packed with not even standing room for some worshippers who had to shelter from the rain under a makeshift corrugated iron porch. The leader of the Good News Church said that he had about one hundred and thirty people coming to his meetings on a Sunday. There must have been more than one thousand at this Catholic charismatic service held on a working day, so as not to interfere with the normal Sunday worship.

The service was called a retreat, but the congregation certainly hadn't come for the peace and quiet of a normal Christian retreat. The worshippers had been fasting since the night before and were now three hours into the service but their enthusiasm was undiminished. We squeezed into the church through a side door, and stood squashed against the wall. The short break had just ended and a young man wearing an open-necked shirt with a guitar strapped over his shoulder had taken up position on one side of the altar on which two red candles flickered. Between the candles the blessed sacrament was exposed in a monstrance looking like a golden sun with rays shooting out of it.

The evangelist waited until the excited murmuring died down and silence settled on the church, then raising his arms he cried, 'Hallelujah, hallelujah, hallelujah!' Hundreds of hands clapped and hundreds of voices responded, 'Hallelujah, hallelujah, hallelujah!' The evangelist cried out again, 'Jesus I come to praise you, I need you! You have been so good to us. You have done such wonders in our life.' Then strumming on his guitar he sang, 'We are here to praise you, Lord Jesus, let us praise you and sing. We are here to give you the best we can bring.' The congregation listened with rapt attention, some hands were folded in the traditional Christian pose for prayer, some were held palms up, and some were cupped. The evangelist started to speak again, urgently, pleading, beseeching, 'Sweet Jesus, I want to walk in your footsteps. Oh Jesus, I need you. Sweet Jesus, it all comes from you. Show me the way I want to tread on your footpath.'

He spoke sometimes in Konkani and sometimes in English. A woman next to us with a cross tattooed at the base of her thumb and wearing a mangalsutra, like the necklace worn by married Hindu women, threw her arms in the air and shouted 'Hallelujah!' The evangelist moved on to country and western style singing 'One day at a time, sweet Jesus, that's all I'm asking of you.' This time the congregation joined in. The excitement mounted. Pinpoints of light from electric candles glittered in the golden reredos. The figure of the Virgin Mary, surrounded by glowing bulbs, looked down on the congregation. All the colours of the rainbow brightened the dimly lit church – mauve, blue, bright green, rose red, canary-yellow saris, skirts, blouses. They were offset by some traditional black churchgoing dresses. The men were less colourful and fewer in number.

The frenzied evangelist cried, 'Wash us, keep us clean, we pray to you, Lord Jesus, hallelujah, hallelujah, hallelujah!' His voice boomed louder and louder, and the congregation joined him in a great crescendo. Then the diminuendo started, the hallelujahs grew softer and softer until they died away in a last whisper. The evangelist proclaimed, 'You are healed,' and a young bearded priest, wearing a simple white vestment with just a plain cross on it, sprinkled holy water on some worshippers crowded round the altar. I assumed they were sick but from our vantage, or disadvantage point, it was impossible to tell.

A healer, a slight, elderly woman with a headscarf tied firmly underneath her chin, took over the microphone and called on members of the congregation to confirm reports of past miracles. She asked a woman to confirm that her backache had been cured. Someone else had been cured of 'a white discharge', but when the healer announced that a patient suffering from blood cancer had been healed there was no confirmation from the congrega-tion. Eventually a woman stood up and said, 'She can't be here today.'

The evangelist took charge again, leading the singing of 'Jesus loves me, that's enough . . .' All around us, young and old, clapped and swayed in time with the music. They sang, 'I am happy today

in Jesus, I am clapping today in Jesus, I am singing today in Jesus.'
The priest lifted the monstrance above his head in a triumphant
gesture, not unlike a tennis champion holding a trophy on high.
The clapping, the singing, the hallelujahs, it seemed would never
end, but eventually the priest put the monstrance down, moved to
the centre of the altar and started the celebration of the mass. The
traditional hushed reverence of the church was restored until after
the epistle when a gospel hymn aroused another frenzy of hallelujahs and the priest was lost in a forest of clapping hands. But as he
opened the prayer book to read the Gospel those hands fluttered
across chests in the sign of the cross and the singing ceased.

The priest preached an unemotional sermon in Konkani warning
the congregation that they must bear witness to Christ in their lives.
It was no good being humble only inside church, they had to
render service to others, to forgive others, to be humble when they
walked outside. That was witnessing to Christ. After the sermon
the priest asked whether anyone had any sins to confess. One
woman we couldn't see properly raised her hand and said, 'I am not
applying the word of God in my own life and I am sorry.' A penitent
standing right by the altar had failed to bear witness because of his
own weaknesses. After each confession the priest said, 'We have
acknowledged our faults, we want to come back to you, please
forgive us.' The bread and the wine were then consecrated, the
communion distributed and a strangely subdued congregation left
the church.

We went to find the priest, Father Agnelo Fernandes, who turned
out to be a Pilar father standing in for the parish priest who was in
Britain on a preaching tour. Father Agnelo had been hearing
confessions since eight in the morning and had only joined the
service towards the end. When I suggested that the service had been
a little unorthodox, he replied, 'We cannot just go on the old way,
that will be the end of the church because this is what the people
want, and if we don't give it, they will go to the Believers.'

'So what is the difference between what you are doing and the
Believers? You are both charismatics surely?'

'Ours is Catholic, you saw for yourself the mass, and I am

here, a priest, to ensure it's Catholic. All the people are Catholic charismatics.'

The next day I found myself in much more sober surroundings – the Archbishop's Palace, which was built on the highest point in Panaji to signify the status of the archbishop in Portuguese Goa. Even now the chief minister's official residence is lower down the hillside. I was met in the courtyard of the long, white, two-storeyed building by a priest who showed me inside. The grandeur of the spacious entrance hall was marred by a bucket in the middle of the floor catching drips from the leaking ceiling. Obviously the church was having difficulty in keeping the archbishop in the style his Portuguese predecessors had enjoyed. The priest accompanied me to the archbishop's study on the first floor, knocked on the door and left me to enter on my own as soon as he heard 'Come in.'

I had seen the photo of the archbishop in our well-thumbed directory of his archdiocese. He looked very much the prelate, with purple buttons on his white cassock and a purple skullcap covering his grey hair. When I entered his office he was sitting at his desk with a large crucifix behind him. The windows were open, there was no stuffy air-conditioning. I had expected an awe-inspiring figure, but he was shorter than I'd imagined and instead of the severe face scowling from the cover of the directory I was greeted with a broad smile and escorted to a comfortable chair. Mediterranean hospitality had survived in his palace, and although it was well before lunch I was offered a drink and a choice of prawn patties or beef sausage rolls. The archbishop was surprised, and perhaps even a little disappointed, when I settled for coffee and a piece of sweet Goan cake known as bebinca. The archbishop drank coffee too.

He wore a silver crucifix round his neck but that was the only sign of his high office. The buttons on his cassock were mother-of-pearl and his curly grey hair was uncovered. Educated in Portuguese throughout his days in the minor seminary, he spoke English with a trace of a Portuguese accent.

He was gratified by the results of his twenty-eight years in charge of the archdiocese, but did not take credit for this himself. When I asked how the church in Goa was flourishing, when in the West it seemed to be in decline, he replied, 'The finger of God.'

'Nothing more?' I asked.

'Well, yes. The people's participation is much better. Then also we used to be very keen on Eucharistic devotion. Of course we still are, but we are also keen on the Bible now.'

'Is it true that St Francis Xavier never carried a Bible with him during all those years of missionary activity?'

'Maybe, maybe, but those were different days. The church has even changed greatly in my short life, and I am very pleased about the laity's participation. You know the small Christian communities we are setting up, they now take it in turns to prepare the mass on Sundays, decide the hymns and the theme and the readings. That would have been impossible when we priests ran everything.'

But when I told him that I had been very impressed by the charismatic service, I could see we were moving on to less sure ground.

'Where was the service?' he asked.

'In the parish church at Mandur.'

'Ah now, I'm not at all sure that is one that our diocesan charismatic service team has approved. I think it's still under review. We have set the team up to control the movement. There is a danger that it will undermine the parish churches, draw people away from their own churches. That's why I have said the charismatic retreats can't be held on Sundays. Your service wasn't on Sunday?' he asked anxiously.

'No, on Friday,' I assured him and he nodded saying, 'Good, good.'

The archbishop was particularly concerned about the healing at charismatic services. 'We don't want people to go to these services and ask for things. We want them to bear witness to God's will,' he said. 'What's particularly worrying is the misuse of the sacrament in healing. There have even been reports of people being force-fed with the sacrament.'

At that stage, I didn't think I would tell him about the use of the monstrance in Mandur, and so I moved the conversation forward, suggesting that the charismatic movement might become so strong it could dictate its own terms for remaining within the church.

'Oh, no, no, no, no,' he replied hurriedly. 'No one can tell where the spirit will blow, and the church must be open to the spirit. But if you read history you will see that there have been many such movements in the past and the church has contained them. Take St Francis, even the Pope didn't quite know whether he should approve of him. He did and now we have Franciscans everywhere including here, and they are doing very good work and are not a worry to me.'

'Well, I hear that you will be getting rid of the worries you have soon, because you are retiring in two years' time. Is that true?'

He leant back in his chair and smiled, 'I will be seventy-five and so I will have done enough, won't I?'

'Yes, I'm sure you will have.'

'As I told you, I have seen many changes and they haven't all been easy for me, educated as I was in a very different tradition. So it is time for a rest, or maybe a change would be a better word because I want to remain active in some way.'

I came away with the impression that the charismatic movement was one change too many for the archbishop, and that he would be very glad to hand that problem over to someone else.

On the last Sunday we met another priest who had not found change easy. When we were sitting in a pew waiting for mass to start in Old Goa's Se Cathedral, a small, elderly but remarkably spry priest came up to us wearing not the usual white cassock but an old-fashioned, tight-fitting black one with a traditional high dog-collar. He asked whether I was a Portuguese speaker and when I told him I didn't know a word of the language he said, 'I usually ask foreigners that because I love speaking Portuguese but I don't get much chance nowadays.'

I asked why the exterior of his cathedral was now yellow instead of the traditional Goan white and this provoked a diatribe against the

Archaeological Survey of India which had taken over responsibility from the church for the monuments of Old Goa. 'We can't do anything to our own cathedral now,' he fumed, hopping from one foot to the other in his anger. 'We even have to get permission to put up a new collection box, and what do they do to preserve the church? Nothing.' As evidence he took me to the west end and showed me piles of rubble where the plaster was peeling from the pillars.

I had noticed that his cassock had purple piping and purple buttons so I asked, 'Does the purple mean you are a monsignor?'

'No. But I am Father Adolpho Joviano Castro Viegas, a canon of the cathedral and the parish priest and that is just as senior.'

Having been put straight about that, I went on to ask, 'In the cathedral, do you keep up the old traditions of worship?'

'Of course I try to, but what can we do? We don't have money to pay for the choirs and all that you need for proper ritual, and the bishop doesn't care either. The Portuguese bishop used to come here regularly with full pomp and devotion. The present one only comes about four times a year. I love the full ritual and singing, it lifts your heart.'

The peppery priest then left me to robe for the chapter mass.

The vast cathedral was far from full when Father Adolpho and six other equally elderly canons entered through the south aisle. Robed in splendid green copes they walked in a solemn procession, accompanied by just one server, to the altar at the top of the chancel steps. Six of the canons including Adolpho took their seats in high-backed chairs behind the altar and one stood at the altar to celebrate the mass with dignity and solemnity. He was accompanied by a small choir in the organ loft.

Looking at the magnificent gilded reredos crowned by the figure of Christ on the cross just below the white-barrelled ceiling of the sanctuary, I couldn't help but think of the Portuguese who had built this monument to impress Goans with the majesty of a God who lived on high. I knew that the church had to change, to bring God down to earth, if it was to survive in independent India, but I also acknowledged that I came from the old tradition, the tradition

Father Adolpho was preserving. I found it easier to worship God in majesty, rather than God the social worker who battles for the poor, or God the personal pal of the charismatics.

this: to teach philosophy to the West and learn its science, to impart purity of life to Europe and attain to her loftier political ideal, to inculcate spirituality to the American mind and acquire the business ways of her merchants.' But in the end Inayat Khan's body was laid to rest in Nizamuddin, where for him it had all started with the Sufism of his native country, India. Today, behind the ancient dargah of Nizamuddin you will find a modern mausoleum dedicated to the twentieth-century saint, and if you are there on a Friday evening you will probably find some members of Farid's family performing qawwali.

Farmer's Reward

On the night of 4 February 2001 Ningappa Basappa Hiregannavar, a thirty-five-year-old farmer, told his wife that he was going out to discuss the family's financial plight with one of the elders of the village of Javur in the southern state of Karnataka. His wife, who was sitting on the earthen floor of the shack they lived in, said nothing, just continuing to breastfeed their third child. Golden maize, still unhusked, lay piled up in one corner, a continuous reminder to the husband and the wife of the crisis they were facing.

Ningappa came from one of the more prosperous families in the village. His father had owned thirty-two acres but, after his death, the family had split up, and the land had been divided between his three sons. Ningappa had moved out of the family house and for the last seven years had been living in this shack. Wooden beams supported a slightly sloping tiled roof, the walls consisted of corrugated iron sheeting and, when Ningappa had run out of that, he had made do with maize straw. He had inherited part of the family debt when the brothers separated, and since then low prices or poor crops had driven him further into the hands of moneylenders. Now he was desperate because he couldn't even sell his maize. There was no demand in the market and he didn't believe the government would bother to buy from a farmer as small as he was.

The village elder's shop was just opposite the home where Ningappa had lived until the family broke up, very much a pukka house, built of bricks with a thick coating of mud for insulation. Although it was nine o'clock, the village elder, Mahabaleshwar Mallappa Desai, was still doing good business, and so the farmer wandered around the lanes of the village. Returning at ten o'clock, he found there were still customers and so he continued his meandering until the shop emptied and he could sit down and confide in Mahabaleshwar.

'We are all in debt, farmers are everywhere,' the elder comforted him. 'I have bigger debts than you do.'

'But my debts just keep growing,' Ningappa sobbed, 'and what hope do I have now of ever providing my family with somewhere to live? I feel disgraced, I have nowhere to show my face, living as I do. I come from a respectable family and my wife and children are reduced to living in a hut.'

Mahabaleshwar tried to calm him. 'It's a matter of patience. These things come round in circles. I am older than you are, I've seen it all before – two or three bad years and then a good one or two, but we never get out of debt, nor do the moneylenders want us to. We survive and so do they.' Leaning forward he patted Ningappa on the face and said, 'Come on, you must be a man. Crying won't help you.'

But Ningappa wasn't going to be consoled. In a voice still choked he replied, 'There's no point in my surviving. My family would be better off if I killed myself, at least the government would have to pay compensation and they would have some money.'

Mahabaleshwar didn't take this threat very seriously and, seeing that there was no way of helping the farmer in his present mood, made no attempt to restrain him when he got up and walked out into the darkness. Shortly afterwards he heard a young man running through the village shouting, 'Come quickly! There's someone trying to drown himself in the tank.'

The whole village rushed to the tank but in the dark no one could see any sign of the farmer. Some men mounted guard on the tank, others fanned out into the fields to search for him, but it wasn't until after dawn that a village boy found Ningappa hanging from a tree. His noose was a cotton lungi.

Ningappa's suicide was only one of several such stories we were told about in Karnataka, one of India's more prosperous and better administered states. In the village of Sutagatti for instance, not far from Hubli, the second largest town in the state, a young and heavily indebted farmer called Irayya Basayya Mukhashivayyanavar had killed himself. We were directed to the house of his uncle.

We found the women of the family sitting on a platform under the porch of their house shaking wheat grains in winnowing baskets. Tamarind pods were spread out to dry at their feet. I broke one open and sucked the tart pulp inside which is one of the main ingredients in south Indian cooking and reputed to have many medicinal qualities. Two stick figures, not unreminiscent of Lowry, painted on the wall, held up a white lingam of Shiva on an ochre background. The lingam was flanked by serpents, symbols of fertility and ancestor worship. This kind of folk painting has been described by one art historian as timeless. A long discussion between the artist, one of the women winnowing wheat, and our interpreter never quite clarified which festival she had painted it for.

News of our arrival was not long in reaching the head of the household, Basayya, who came hurrying up the lane wearing a long white kurta and dhoti. His forehead bore the three white lines of a worshipper of Shiva, his hair was uncombed, his grey beard might have been stubble or might have been intentional, and his walrus moustache lacked any precision. He could have been taken for a deliberately dishevelled holy man, but he was a working farmer.

Basayya took us across the road to the house of his nephew Irayya, the farmer who had committed suicide, and introduced us to his family. A younger brother sat glumly against some sacks of grain saying nothing. His mother and sister were no more communicative. So it was left to the uncle to tell us what had happened.

This was another case of a joint family splitting up, leaving thirty-two-year-old Irayya, the youngest of the brothers, with just two and a half acres. He had sown potatoes, cotton and maize but a small river flooded his land in heavy rains and his crop was destroyed. He tried again with *jowar*, or sorghum, but once more the rain went against him and the yield was only two sacks of grain. 'There was a weed problem too,' the older farmer said, 'and then there was the well too. That turned into bad luck because other farmers went in for borings and so the level of the water under the ground sank and his well dried up.'

'Did he give any warning that he might commit suicide?' I asked.

'No. He was discussing his wedding and his brother's, both were planned, so it looked as though he had the intention to live a normal life, and then one day we found him hanging in the shed he'd built near his land.'

In the dead farmer's pocket was a list of all his debts. They included money the village accountant, a minor official, was demanding before he would register the transfer of Irayya's share of the family land.

'The village accountant has been suspended,' said Basayya, 'but what good does that do now? It won't bring our boy back. Compensation has been paid too, but that won't bring him back either.'

The government had given a hundred thousand rupees, a local minister ten thousand, and Karnataka's only former prime minister, Deve Gowda, who at the time was trying to make a political comeback, another ten.

As we rose to leave, I asked our interpreter to explain how distressed we were by this story, and to offer our deepest sympathy. The family of the dead farmer just folded their hands and didn't even say 'namaste'. No attempt was made to detain us for the traditional hospitality shown to guests. But Basayya insisted that we should go back to his house where we were given *poha*, savoury pounded yellow rice, and sweet tea.

Our interpreter, Hemant Kumar Panchal, wore a green khadi shawl wherever he went, the emblem of the farmers' movement which had rocked Karnataka in the eighties, but he was not a farmer by birth. He was one of the many Indians who are still prepared to sacrifice the prospect of 'the good life' for what they see as the cause of their country. I have found them in many different places, struggling for all sorts of causes. Hemant I had first met when he came to Delhi to discuss restarting the farmers' movement, but on an all-India basis this time.

Hemant's father, Dr Y. C. Panchal, was a distinguished professor of crop physiology who had spent most of his life teaching and researching in the agricultural university of the town of Dharwar, not many miles away from the villages we were visiting. His was a very strict upbringing. 'My mother was a great disciplinarian,' he told me as we drove away from Sutagatti, 'a dictator in the house.

We had servants but she made me wash my own clothes and clean my utensils myself.'

The strictness paid off and Hemant passed the highly competitive entrance exam for the prestigious Indian Institute of Technology in Chennai, which was Madras at that time. A German professor, on a temporary teaching assignment there, once told me he wished his students back home were half as good as the students in Chennai.

Engineering is considered one of the most promising careers in India, but Hemant wasn't tempted by stories of large salaries and opportunities abroad. He gave up university because he wanted 'to work for farmers'.

This, he told me, had not been well received at home. 'There was a hue and cry in the house. It was very difficult to cope with my parents at that time but somehow I passed through it.'

Where did this philanthropic urge come from? While at school Hemant had met boys who were connected with left-wing underground movements. They wanted him to join, and he admitted he had been 'slightly attracted to the ultras'. But he came to the conclusion that the underground movements, Marxists for the most part, 'lacked social roots and total strength'. He felt they didn't belong to the countryside, and were propagating an alien ideology unsuitable for India. He smiled. 'All my friends laughed at me. They said revolution wasn't brought by the people but by activists. But I still couldn't draw out from them what they wanted to do apart from be anti-government, and somehow I felt if I wanted to achieve anything I would have to get close to the people.'

Hemant's views were strengthened by reading Gandhi. It was from him that he learnt how 'to face villagers and get on with them'.

Reading is one thing and putting it into practice is another. When Hemant, just eighteen years old, did buy ten acres of land in a remote part of northern Karnataka and go off to 'become part of a village', all his friends thought village life would be too tough for him and expected him back in Bangalore within two months, but he is still farming that land himself.

Once he was accepted in the village and felt at home there, he joined the farmers' movement and soon became accepted as a leader. He was now taking us to a village, Morab, where he said the farmers were particularly active. He had called a meeting so that we could get a first-hand account of the problems they were facing.

Morab was obviously a village which commanded clout because, although its population was only ten thousand, it had a branch of the Vijaya Bank in the main square whose signboard proclaimed that it was wholly owned by the government of India. Opposite was the Panchayat Bhavan, the concrete box which housed the offices of the village council. Inside about forty farmers were waiting to meet us, among them were at least two Muslims. We were taken to the top of the table where the most important people were seated. On my right was the secretary of the council, an official of the government who was the only member of the village elite not wearing traditional clothes. Next to him was the elected head of the panchayat. On my left there was a member of the district council, a farmer who owned fifty acres. There were boards on the wall bearing the names of the members of the panchayat committees, some of whom, including the vice-president of the panchayat, were women. When we asked why none of the women had come to the meeting we were told they were busy at home, indicating that perhaps they were just there to fulfil the quotas required by the law and that real power still lay with their menfolk. A blackboard listed details of the work in progress under the supervision of the council – pukka instead of mud flooring for the houses of twenty-two Dalit families, a drain for the road which runs alongside the temple, improvements to the school, and a veterinary hospital.

Hemant stood to open the proceedings. Stroking his wispy black beard and adjusting his green shawl, he thought for a moment or two before starting to explain our mission. Although by no means substantial in size, he commanded the farmers' attention. After embarrassing me by exaggerating my influence and importance, he told the farmers, 'No politicians pay attention to our problems, and the bureaucrats are entirely against us so it's very important to get the help of the press. We must put our problems to them.'

There was no embarrassed silence when he opened the meeting

to the farmers, inviting them to tell us about their problems. Voices from all round the table told us that prices were below production costs, the market had collapsed, and the government was doing nothing. A farmer standing at the far end of the hall shouted, 'We harvested the maize in October and we still can't find a market for it six months later.'

When I asked about the government's decision to enter the market, buy in a big way, and so, hopefully, raise the price of maize, there was a chorus of protests.

'They haven't procured a tenth of the crop.'

'You mean a twentieth.'

'The government does unscientific purchasing, they haven't succeeded in raising the price in the market.'

'There's no profit for us in the government price, and the market means a definite loss.'

'The big farmers in the village will see that their produce gets taken up by the government, but if you only have forty quintals what hope is there for you?'

Hemant managed to restore some order, and the meeting turned into a veiled attack on Mr Hanchinal, the prosperous farmer sitting at the top of the table with me. There were complaints that big farmers were able to rig the markets and ensure that the government procured their produce first.

'They are not really farmers,' said a young man whose crumpled kurta contrasted with the sleek appearance of Mr Hanchinal. 'They are farmers–cum–merchants.'

'Merchants–cum–farmers, you mean,' interjected his neighbour, looking hard at Mr Hanchinal, who smiled wearily, acknowledging that he was a target, but said nothing.

An elderly man, sharp-featured and with wily eyes who had been anxious to speak for some time held up his hand again, and Hemant invited him to have his say. He proceeded to give a lengthy lecture, replete with convoluted phraseology, on scientific pricing. I was not surprised to learn that he was a lawyer-cum-farmer. It eventually transpired that scientific pricing meant farmers should get costs plus twenty-five per cent.

Mr Hanchinal intervened for the first time. 'Although a guaranteed price is what we need, we will never get it. But what we can demand is a bigger market, and that means exports. The government doesn't even announce its import–export policy until after the crops are handed to the merchants. There should be no restrictions on exports, but of course there should be restrictions on imports. I have been told that the World Bank has been very critical of the government's ban on exports and the way they annouce their export policies so late.'

No one told him that the World Bank would certainly not approve of a ban on imports either and the debate returned to the government's grain procurement policy. The lawyer re-entered the fray, complaining that his maize had been stuck for twenty days at the procurement centre. Every day he had to go there, and to look after his grain he had to employ a watchman round the clock.

'The delay in lifting from the farmers is because they are waiting for a bribe,' he explained.

Another farmer added, 'Yes, and if you bribe you will get your cheque quicker too.'

Hemant then raised the question of credit. Few Indian farmers have cash flows adequate to provide for the purchase of their seeds, fertilizers, and other inputs. They have to borrow each sowing season. When Indira Gandhi nationalized the banks more than thirty years ago, one of the reasons she gave was to provide rural credit so that farmers did not fall into the hands of loan sharks. The local branch of the Vijaya Bank should have been doing just that. But the farmers were united in their condemnation of the banking system. All complained that the procedures for raising a loan were so cumbersome and time-consuming that the money arrived well after it was needed. So, in spite of Indira Gandhi, farmers still went to private moneylenders even though they charged four per cent interest a month plus a one per cent surcharge. One farmer said there were twenty private financiers flourishing in Morab village alone. Another whispered into Hemant's ear, 'There's one over there, sitting next to your guest.'

Mr Hanchinal did not rise in defence of private finance.

Hemant then spoke for some time on the need for farmers to unite if they were to press their demands effectively. He spoke quietly, his hands folded in front of him. There was no rhetoric, no gesturing, none of the tricks of the orator's trade, but he held their attention as he reminded them of the heyday of the farmers' movement when the government had really been shaken, and of the defeat they had inflicted on a chief minister in the election to the state assembly. But after the speech was over one of the farmers said, 'The movement depended on emotions aroused by the police firing on us when we were demonstrating. That sort of emotional reaction cannot last for long.'

For some reason this brought another farmer to the subject of drink. 'Liquor complicates matters,' he said. 'Poor farmers turn to liquor. They earn forty rupees a day and then spend it on liquor so they are weakened. Small farmers are addicted to this because of tension.'

On cue, a drunken farmer who had been ejected from the hall twice, staggered in for the third time. The meeting broke up with Mr Hanchinal trying to restrain his colleagues who had grabbed the drunk and were frogmarching him out of the hall, cuffing him around the head to help him on his way.

The village seemed to be drowning in maize, pile after pile of golden grain waiting to be bagged, the tissue-paper-thin dried sheaths of the corn cobs littering every lane. As we left Morab, we passed a mechanical thresher producing yet more grain. The rattle of the machine turned to a roar each time a basket of corn cobs was poured into its mouth. A chain of girls passing the baskets from one to the other kept its hunger at bay. The farmer, who was not taking an active role in all this, was a surly, silent man who rebuffed our efforts to discuss prices and discover why his threshing was so long delayed.

We drove down what is known as a village road, in reality not much more than a potholed cart track, past some of the varied crops of northern Karnataka. Hemant commented on the cost of bad roads to farmers, increasing transport expenses and damaging vehicles even as uncomplicated as bullock carts. A white-eyed buzzard swooped dramatically over the fields of tall jowar whose leaves were turning brown as the harvest approached. A few black leaves still hung from the dismal stalks of sunflowers already harvested. We stopped to pick – steal would I suppose be a more appropriate word – some green *channa*, or chickpeas, and to look at a field of golden safflower, a crop I couldn't remember seeing before. Hemant explained it could only be harvested at dawn when the dew had softened the prickly plants. That might have been one reason why it hadn't caught on in the way he thought it should have done, because it was sturdy, resistant to drought and pests, and produced an excellent edible oil.

Before we reached a tarmacked road, we came upon a farmer who was willing to discuss the maize crop. He, his son, and his wife were working in the middle of a field, without any protection from the sun, shovelling grain into sacks. We took them to the shade of a tamarind tree to discuss the economics of their harvest.

Hemant had invited Dr Rajendra Poddar, a young agricultural economist to travel with us. Dapper in his light-blue shirt with button-down collar and dark-blue trousers, he looked out of place beside the farmer in his sweat-stained, frayed white shirt and dhoti. The farmer's son was only wearing a lungi tucked up above his knees and a vest. But the economist was not an armchair or air-conditioned academic. He had come up the hard way. His father was a farmer who could barely read and write, but had the enterprise to be the first person in his district to irrigate his land, thereby transforming the culture of the surrounding villages, which had previously depended on rain-fed agriculture.

After detailed questioning in which Dr Poddar used the skill of an economist and the knowledge of a farmer, he drew up a balance sheet of the maize crop which showed that the expenditure, including interest at five per cent a month on the crop loan, was 6150 rupees per acre, and income from the sale of the grain was 3960 rupees. So the net loss per acre was 2190 rupees. As the farmer had sown eight acres of maize, his total loss was 17,520 rupees. His income would have been higher if he had gone to the government procurement centre, instead of selling to a private trader at a hundred rupees a sack less than the official price, but the farmer, rubbing his head covered with thick grey hair, explained, 'Nobody cares if you go to the government. At least with the private trader I get my money at once and it's much easier. I don't have to take my grain anywhere either. He comes and collects it.'

His son added, 'It's probably more profitable too, what with all the interest we would have to pay while we waited for our money from the government.'

'That would be less if you'd borrowed from the bank,' Dr Poddar pointed out.

But the farmer had an answer to that too. 'We couldn't. We already had a debt of 23,000 rupees with the State Bank of India, which meant no other bank would have lent to us.'

So what was the point of farming if you were going to make a loss? For the farmer it wasn't just money that counted. 'Owning land is a matter of prestige and it would be a disgrace if you didn't farm it. When our joint family broke, I only actually owned 2.3 acres of land, but to keep up my standing as a farmer I have leased nearly 6 acres. Now I find my son and I have to work elsewhere to have money for household needs.'

'Do you mean labouring?' asked Dr Poddar.

'Yes, sometimes on bigger farmers' land, sometimes whatever we can get.'

'How can you go on like this? You are losing money.'

'I have hopes. The last two years have been very bad, maybe the prices will improve next year.'

'What about your debts?'

'I will use the money from this crop to pay the moneylender and the bank can wait. Everyone owes money to the banks here, and there's no disgrace in that. If they want to take my land, we'll see what happens. It's not that easy for them.'

Much to the disgust of Hemant and Dr Poddar, our first night in northern Karnataka had been spent in one of those modern Indian hotels whose management hoped that fancy sanitary ware would disguise faulty plumbing. Hemant had booked us into the guest house of the Dharwar Agricultural University where his father had taught and Dr Poddar had studied, but we had lost our room to the state agricultural commissioner and his entourage. Hemant and Dr Poddar were determined that this evening we would arrive there in time to secure our accommodation. However their determination conflicted with Hemant's insistence that we fulfil a schedule which all our lengthy discussions had delayed beyond any hope of completion. In the end we compromised by postponing a visit to Hemant's own village, but we still arrived at the university well after dark.

The next morning we went to see the much-criticized procurement arrangements for ourselves at the Amargol branch of the Karnataka State Warehousing Corporation.

Queues of trucks and tractors, waiting to pass over the one and only weighbridge, stretched the entire length of the warehouses and disappeared behind them. There were more queues on the main road outside. On the verandah of the warehouse office farmers jostled each other to get their documents recorded by just one bald-headed, bad-tempered clerk. They also had to register their vehicles with the police for some reason the sub-inspector on duty was unable to explain.

A crowd, anxious to express their frustration, gathered around us. Some had been waiting for twenty-four hours to complete the complicated process which involved queuing first to get their loaded vehicles weighed, then queuing to get them unloaded, and finally joining a third queue to have their empty vehicles weighed, and all this was only the end of the story. All the farmers complained of long waits, one as long as two months, at local procurement centres before they were allowed to bring their maize to these warehouses.

A young farmer, who was also a transporter, was particularly vocal. 'They should have started procurement here months ago,' he insisted. 'They have only just started buying, and the rate they are going most of the grain will start losing quality. If it's not properly stored it loses quality after six months.'

'Why do you think they have only started buying recently?' I asked.

Back without any hesitation came the reply: 'Those suicide reports. Only when they face a crisis do politicians get worried.'

Gilly focused her camera on him but he put his hand across his face. She said there was no danger of the photograph being seen on television, but he was not reassured.

All this maize was an embarrassment to the central government. It already had a massive stock of grain. One economist had recently calculated that if all the sacks stored by the government's Food Corporation of India were lined up they would stretch for a million miles. Yet millions of children in India are still chronically under-nourished, and the government itself admits that thirty-six per cent of the wheat it allots to those who need subsidized food doesn't reach them. It gets eaten by insects and rats, or falls into the hands of private traders.

The Amargol warehouses were already stacked to capacity, and so the grain was now being unloaded down the road in what had once been a factory for manufacturing gears. The business must have failed because there was no sign of any machinery, and the factory had become a gigantic barn fast filling up with sacks of maize. An official who was meant to be grading grain was fast asleep at his desk. One group of coolies was sitting on the floor eating lunch. Another group was slowly unloading a lorry. Three men, bare-chested with their backs protected by cotton cloth knotted over their heads, laboured to lift a sack weighing ninety-six kilogrammes on to the back of a fourth coolie. He tottered precariously across the uneven terrain of the grain mountain and threw the sack down, yanking it into place with a grappling hook, reminiscent of the longshoremen in *On the Waterfront*. The hook tore the sack and grain dribbled out. It was obvious that, contrary to the principles of good inventory management, the first grain to be stored, the bottom of the mountain, would be the last to go out of the warehouse. But the Food Corporation doesn't have to bother with those sort of considerations because its costs are subsidized by the government, and it faces no competition.

The banking system, we were to discover, was no less antiquated and inefficient – the farmers' complaints about credit were as justified as their criticism of the procurement system we saw at Amargol. Hemant and Dr Poddar took us to meet the manager of the Malaprabha Grameen (or rural) Bank in Navalgund, a town where police opened fire for the first time at the height of the farmers' movement in which Hemant had played a prominent role.

The branch was a narrow room on the ground floor of a small house. Into it were crowded the clerks, the counter, and the benches where farmers waited for clerical complexities to be unravelled. The manager had no office of his own but sat at the entrance. Behind him were the safes. The wooden notice on his desk identified the manager as 'K. G. Ballarwad, Bachelor of Science, Bachelor of Law'. A small man, greyed by twenty-two years drudgery in the bank, I felt certain that he would be bound by rules which prohibited him from talking to the press. But not at all – he was most polite and very communicative.

He agreed that the process for getting a loan was somewhat complicated and could put off potential borrowers, especially if they were not very well educated. He counted the obstacles a borrower had to negotiate on his fingers.

'Before he can even ask for a loan he has to produce, one – land records, two – records of rights, three – no dues from the government, four – records of all land revenue paid, five – no dues certificates from other banks, six – land valuation certificates, seven – no dues from agricultural societies, and if he is a minor, permission from the court.'

'How does he show he doesn't owe money to any bank?' I asked.

'He goes to each bank to get a certificate.'

'How many is that?'

'Seven commercial banks and two cooperative banks.'

'Nine altogether,' I said in amazement. 'He has to go to nine different banks.'

'Yes, I suppose nine, and even after all these safeguards our recovery rate is only fifty-five per cent.'

'Fifty-five per cent, you mean nearly half the loans go down the drain?'

'If you put it like that, yes. It can be worse than that. We had to move this branch to Navalgund from the village where it was established because non-payment was eighty-five to ninety-five per cent.'

A clerk pushed a heavy, bound ledger in front of the manager – The Register of Cheques, Bills, and Drafts Deposited for Collection. He signed the entry in the ledger, opened an ink pad and stamped the cheque that went with it, explaining that he had to sign every transaction, which meant a thousand signatures a day.

'But don't you have any other supervisory staff?' I asked.

'Yes,' he replied, 'I have two who are classified supervisory staff, but under the bank rules they are not allowed to supervise.'

Mr Ballarwad was neither a faceless nor a heartless bureaucrat. He realized that the complexities of the banking system drove farmers into the hands of the moneylenders. 'In our area we are trying to stop private lending,' he said, 'but farmers are in the habit of taking private loans. When the bank loan is overdue they will go to the private financier to get money to repay it.'

Dr Poddar quoted an unnamed British author who had written: 'The Indian farmer is born in debt, lives in debt and dies in debt.'

'Is reborn in debt too,' added Hemant.

We had asked Hemant to introduce us to one or two of the teachers at the agricultural university but I was horrified when, on our way back to Dharwar, he told me the vice-chancellor was going to round up all his professors to meet us. There was no getting out of it, so the next morning we walked down the wooded hill from the guest house, with the neatly set out fields of experimental crops below us, to the administrative building which dominated the campus. Indo-Palladian in style and crowned with a dome, it gave the impression of some seat of classical learning rather than the headquarters of a comparatively new agricultural university. We walked up the stairs to a large room where some sixty academics sat round a U-shaped table waiting to hear me speak. I protested that as a mere Bachelor of Arts with no research behind me in any subject, I had no right to address an assembly of scholars. I wanted to learn from them, not speak to them. But I did describe briefly the complaints we had heard from farmers and asked what their views were on the agricultural problems of Karnataka.

There seemed to be universal agreement that agricultural research had focused on production and ignored 'post-harvest' problems. One plant physiologist led the breast-beating, 'We forgot the market. Now the stark reality is staring us in the face. Farmers come to us and say, "We did everything you told us to produce crops – now tell us where to sell them." This bitter lesson has only just been learnt.'

But according to an agricultural marketing specialist, it was the farmers' fault for ignoring an obvious fact. 'Every market has an absorption level,' he said. 'They have ignored the consumer base. I have the seeds available and so I sow, have the resources so I grow, a farmer says, but without market there should be no growth at all.'

Several academics then pointed out that there would be a bigger market if there had been more investment in food storage facilities and food processing industries, some of them blaming the government for this. Others criticized the government for a lack of crop forecasting. But the marketing expert interjected to say that farmers and academics alike were too dependent on the government and ought to do more for themselves. He was shot down by a colleague who said, 'No, the government should come in in a big way to help agriculture.'

When Hemant suggested what was needed was 'a model neither capitalist nor socialist', I said, 'That's the holy grail we are all searching for.'

In the end, the vice-chancellor, while not ruling out the role of private capital and initiatives, put much of the blame on the government saying, 'They are on the side of the consumers entirely. All they want is cheap food. Every IAS officer should be made to stay in a village and work with farmers for one year, then the problems will be solved. Only if an IAS officer shows he can run a marginal farm should he be allowed to occupy a secretary to government chair.'

Seniority is still respected in India, and the word 'sir' is frequently to be heard but, comparatively young though he was and junior in the academic hierarchy too, Dr Poddar was not overawed by the vice-chancellor.

'What we have is a problem of localized over-production,' he said, as if pronouncing the final verdict. 'Since the sixties our main emphasis has been on production, but by the eighties we had the problem of supply management and we should have concentrated on that.'

After the meeting in the university we left to fulfil our commitment to Hemant's village. On the way I asked Dr Poddar how there could be a surplus in a country where the government itself admitted that almost one third of the population didn't get enough to eat. The infrastructure, he believed, was part of the problem – not enough effective investment in road construction and maintenance, electricity supply, and storage. Produce wasn't able to move from markets where there was a surplus to those where there was a shortage. The government had made matters worse by restricting movement between states. The history of procurement hadn't been a happy one either. It had failed to guarantee fair prices in surplus situations, much of the food was destroyed in storage, and what did get into the public distribution system didn't reach those who needed it most because of the two inevitable flaws in anything the government did – corruption and inefficiency. But Dr Poddar didn't want to paint 'a totally negative picture'.

'It's not all bad news,' he assured us. 'Indian agricultural scientists have made tremendous contributions. DCH32 cotton, for instance, is a great revolution. Farmers have shown great willingness to try new varieties of seed and new methods too. That is why we face these difficulties now. But the government should have seen this production problem earlier. They have a plan for industry but no plan for agriculture which, although so many people depend on it for their livelihood, has been starved of capital. Even now, with all these World Bank and IMF economic reforms, the emphasis is on industry and commerce, not on agriculture.'

Although Karnataka is thought of as one of India's modernizing states, primitive methods of agriculture still survive. We passed one farmer driving two bullocks round and round in circles pulling a stone roller to thresh wheat. But it was the farmers who were getting the traffic to do the threshing for them that particularly upset Dr Poddar. Their harvested channa was liberally spread over the road so that vehicles would drive over it and separate the chickpeas from their pods.

'Apart from being lazy farming, it's very dangerous to do this on a highway,' he complained. 'Just look at those people squatting in the road and sweeping up the seeds, one of them could easily be run over.' Our driver was not amused either as time and again he was forced to brake by a thick carpet of channa straw.

There was some tarmac on the road leading to Belvatagi, the village where Hemant had bought his land and learned to be a farmer. On the outskirts of the village, Hemant pointed to a comparatively recent plantation of coconut palms and fruit trees, a rare sight in this area with its long tradition of arable farming.

'That's what we should be doing now if traditional crops are failing,' said Hemant. 'Let the farmer be in the field for a challenge rather than waiting for protection.'

But Hemant himself was still very much an arable farmer. Standing in the middle of the six acres of jowar he had planted, he plucked a head which had turned white, and chewed one of the seeds. 'Not quite ripe,' he exclaimed. 'If it was I would have to crunch it, you would hear the crack.' Last year his jowar had fetched 650 rupees a quintal, this year the market rate was only 400.

He pointed to a shami tree explaining, 'That was the tree I ran round when the villagers tested me. They said, if you are a farmer, lift a sack of grain and dump it on a tractor trailer. I lifted the sack, ran away from the tractor round the tree and then back to dump it just to show that I was more than fit to be a farmer. After that I was accepted in the village.'

Hemant had also conducted an experiment in self-sufficiency. He had stayed in a hut on his land and grown what he needed. 'I didn't break down,' he told us, 'and I found I only needed one hundred rupees a month for cash purchases.'

When we reached the village we stopped at a bilious-green, concrete building which doubled as a village hall and temple. The

he insisted that there was never any 'quid pro quo', that money was never accepted for doing favours.

As for Sant Bux, he never recovered from what he saw as his brother's disloyalty. He left Delhi, where his only ambition lay, and returned to his house in Allahabad. There he seemed to lose all interest in life. We didn't know at the time, but his wife told us later that he had collected all his personal papers together in a bundle, given them to a friend and asked him to throw them into the Sangam, the sacred place in Allahabad where the Ganges meets the River Jamuna. He became ill but when we suggested he should come back to Delhi to consult with the best-known doctors, he showed no interest. The last time Gilly saw him before he died, he greeted her with the words, 'Why have you bothered to come and see me?' Tears filled her eyes and she replied, 'If I don't come to see you, who will I come to see?'

Sant Bux had started out with bright prospects but his career failed because he was too honest to flatter, or to ask for favours, even from his brother.

The Water Harvesters

At the beginning of the hot weather in 2000, the Indian media discovered 'the worst drought of the century' – there were even warnings of 'the worst famine of the century'. The drought was 'spreading like an epidemic', and agriculture was 'being pushed over the precipice'. Wells dug as deep as 1500 feet had dried up and so, for the first time, had a reservoir constructed 340 years ago by the Maharaja of Udaipur. 'Cattle-bone dealers have a field day', was one of the more macabre headlines. Women were filmed standing in long queues with brass pots on their heads waiting for water, and disconsolate farmers were interviewed standing on soil baked and cracked like crazy paving. State governments, anxious to squeeze as much money as possible for relief from the central government were jacking up the story too. The international press was not far behind, and it began to look as though the world was facing another calamity.

Within a month, though, most of the media, Indian and international, had lost interest in the drought. Perhaps this was because diligent searches by journalists had only revealed two cases of people who might have died of starvation. Perhaps, to be less cynical, it was because state governments were coping with the immediate consequences of what was certainly a severe water shortage by providing drinking water in tankers and fodder for cattle.

The disappearance of this story prompted me to pick up a remarkable book called *Everybody Likes a Good Drought* which had lain in my to-be-read pile far too long. Written by P. Sainath, an Indian journalist, it is among other things a harsh indictment of the reporting on those who live below the poverty line and the disasters that afflict them. After two years of investigation he came to the conclusion that journalists were only interested in what happened during disasters and in their immediate aftermath, they were not concerned about the causes of the disasters and the possible remedies. Sainath found one report that talked of 'perpetual drought and scarcity conditions' in an area with a more than adequate rainfall. The journalist did not explain how this anomaly had come about. Sainath did – destruction of the traditional irrigation systems, development schemes which did more harm than good, money-lenders, and the failure of land reforms. Sainath blamed a government development policy which had shirked the big issues, like ownership of land, and a development policy which did not involve those it was meant to help – it didn't even seek their consent. This was not widely understood, he maintained, because the mass media were becoming further and further removed from what he called 'mass reality'. But Sainath discerned a new mood among the poor. He wrote, 'In different parts of the country people are asserting themselves against great odds in different ways. In some cases these may not be the healthiest of ways. But all of them represent this reality, the ruled are no longer willing to be ruled in the old way.'

Gujarat in western India was one of the drought-stricken states, it was also the scene of a battle raging over the construction of a dam on the Narmada, the only major Indian river whose waters had not been harnessed. Opponents of the dam saw it as typical of the development policies that Sainath complained about. Without being consulted, thousands and thousands of villagers had lost their land to make way for the reservoir. The enormous cost of the project had left little or no money for reviving traditional methods of irrigation and preserving water. What's more there was a people's movement to stop the dam. Under the leadership of a charismatic woman named Medha Patkar they had succeeded in getting the World Bank to withdraw its support for the dam, and the Japanese government to withdraw a loan, although that decision was reversed. The movement had also forced the courts to take notice of their complaints. At the time of the drought, the judges were about to decide whether the dam could be completed or not.

Gujarat had been the home state of Mahatma Gandhi, the advocate of development by villagers for villagers, and if his influence lives on anywhere, it lives on there. So Gujarat seemed the obvious place to go to test Sainath's theories.

Local journalists are the unsung heroes of most foreign corres-pondents' stories, and so when I arrived in Rajkot, the capital of the Saurashtra region of Gujarat, I made straight for the office of a Saurashtrian paper. The paper was called *Fulchab*, or basket of flowers, a high-minded name for a high-minded paper, a name with a touch of the poetic for a paper whose first editor, Zaverchand Meghani, was described by Mahatma Gandhi as India's national poet. Dinesh Raja, the present editor, keeps large pictures of Zaverchand Meghani and the philanthropic businessman who founded the paper behind his desk. He does not have to bow to any commercial pressures because the paper is still owned by the trust set up by that businessman.

I was not the first person to drop in on Dinesh Raja. I found him presiding, like a benign Buddha, over an assembly of local worthies and some journalists from Ahmedabad, the chief city of Gujarat. All were very anxious to ensure I was correctly briefed on the drought. The most insistent was a man Dinesh Raja introduced as a 'veteran journalist'. Everyone in India has to have a status, a rank in a hierarchy, and in journalism when you graduate from senior to veteran it usually means you have retired. Hemant Pandya with his close-cropped, grey hair, his lean, lined face, his cheeks collapsed because of a lack of teeth, was clearly beyond retirement age, but that hadn't dimmed his energy or his enthusiasm. Determined to have his say first he rose from his chair, turned towards me and, with all the authority of his superior years, began a lecture.

'To understand this drought you have to understand Saurashtra, which is not like other parts of India. Here we say, "A man who doesn't respect the brave and the saints, is not a man at all."'

Seeing that I was not quite getting the connection between sanctity and drought, Dinesh Raja intervened explaining, 'The saints here, instead of advising their followers to retire from the world and live in ashrams as they do elsewhere, or asking for money to build temples, spread the message of social service. The effects of this drought are being mitigated by the tradition of social service the saints left us.'

This prompted the veteran to declaim, 'Service of the people is service of God; all the poor are God.'

I pointed out that this was also the tradition of Mother Teresa of Calcutta, but that was ignored and the lecture continued . . . 'Here the saints were not just upper caste, they came from the backward castes, and the Dalits too who were despised elsewhere. We were more forward a hundred years back.'

Everyone burst into laughter and the old man sat down, satisfied at least for the moment. This gave the editor the chance to tell me about the support the saints of today had given to 'a people's movement' to mitigate Saurashtra's chronic water shortage by reviving traditional methods of 'harvesting water'. Apparently one of the leading saints – a term freely applied to Hindu holy men – had called a meeting of all his fellow religious leaders and told them to teach their followers in the villages that they had been misled by the government, with its emphasis on big new schemes which never 'delivered the goods'. As a result of this 'false propaganda', villagers had come to believe that traditional methods were out of date, too small-scale. The editor went on to say, 'Because of this drought and the people's movement, the villagers are now turning their backs on the government propaganda, and not only that, they're building the check dams and digging the ponds for themselves, not relying on corrupt officials and the contractors who loot the public. What Gandhi had dreamt of, villagers becoming self-sufficient and looking after their own needs, is coming true at last.'

Fulchab had played a role in the people's movement by running a campaign to promote water harvesting. The veteran journalist was determined that I should be aware of this. Leaning forward and jabbing his finger in my direction he proclaimed, 'The awakening of the people has been done here. This paper is the pioneer. It's a mission, a mission.'

The stout, homely Dinesh Raja sitting comfortably behind his desk, looking anything but a fanatic missionary, was content to allow others to take up the story of *Fulchab*'s good works. His former circulation manager, who was now a social worker, explained how *Fulchab* had organized a scheme to deliver water by tanker free of charge to the citizens of Rajkot. Gujaratis are great settlers. Some say as many as forty per cent of the people of Indian origin settled in Britain and forty-five per cent of those in America are from Gujarat. The Gujarati diaspora also spread throughout eastern and southern Africa and the Gulf countries. These prosperous business communities had contributed generously to *Fulchab*'s fund. While I was sitting in his office Dinesh Raja got news that a Gujarati settled in Bahrain had sent a cheque for the equivalent of two thousand pounds.

This prompted yet another outburst from Hemant Pandya. 'I told you. The press you are visiting is a mission. It's a mission which fought for the freedom of the people and now it's fighting for their freedom from the misrule of the rulers.'

Sitting in the offices of *Fulchab*, a paper I am sure Sainath would find less to complain about than most papers, I had been presented with the opportunity to investigate the 'worst drought of the century', to study the remedies and witness the people's rejection of their rulers. The editor of *Fulchab* also provided me with the place to start, the village of Rajsamdhiyala where, he told me, there had been a people's revolution. It had been led by the sarpanch or chairman of the village council.

Dinesh Raja rang the mobile number of the sarpanch, and learnt that he was in Rajkot. Within a matter of minutes he had joined us in the editor's office, and after a brief introduction he said brusquely, 'If you want to see why there is no need for a drought in Gujarat, come with me.'

Two grim, grey, stone towers still guard the gateway of the high school in Rajkot through which Gandhi used to run home as soon as classes were over. He wrote in his autobiography, 'I couldn't bear to talk to anybody, I was even afraid lest anyone should poke fun at me.' A strange beginning for a man who was to become the most prominent and outspoken critic of the politics and economics of his time. Gandhi believed, 'Independence must begin at the bottom. Thus every village will be a republic, or panchayat, having full powers.' So I assumed that the sarpanch who had done just what Gandhi wanted, had turned his village into a republic, would be a follower of his teaching. I was wrong.

Hardevsinh Jadeja wore a bushshirt, trousers, and a smart pair of shoes, not a stitch of *khadi*, the cloth woven by villagers which is the uniform of the Mahatma's followers. Gandhi always travelled by public transport and would never have owned a car. When I suggested we should drive to the village in my car, the sarpanch was somewhat offended that I didn't seem to realize he had a car of his own. A villager with a car and a mobile phone was odd enough in my experience, but worse was to follow from the Gandhian point of view. As he drove with dangerous determination through the traffic of Rajkot, which like all Indian towns didn't seem to have any rules of the road, instead of advocating Gandhi's simplicity of life and austerity, the sarpanch boasted of his own prosperity.

'They are talking of a drought,' he said scornfully. 'I've got a crop of bhindi, and it needs plenty of water. I expect it to fetch me at least eighty thousand rupees, and in these days when other farmers don't have water it might be a lot more – you never can tell with markets, can you?'

Hardevsinh had an M.A. in English from a college in Rajkot, but he didn't have much use for it. Cutting in front of a three-wheeler rickshaw to avoid a lopsided bus, so overcrowded it seemed in imminent danger of toppling over, he said, 'What matters to me is what I've learnt as a farmer. I'm of course a farmer by birth and I just increased my knowledge. My father used to earn one and a half lakhs from his vegetables. Now I earn more than ten, so you can see how much I've learnt.'

Eventually we extricated ourselves from the traffic of Rajkot and emerged on to the Bhavnagar highway where the going was smoother. Bhavnagar is a city to the south-east of Rajkot, on the Gulf of Khambhat. After some twenty kilometres we turned off the highway on to a track which was perfectly motorable but not tarmacked, and drove under a concrete arch inscribed with the words 'Rajsamdhiyala Gram Panchayat'. This was the border between India and the *gram*, or village, whose panchayat, under the

leadership of Hardevsinh Jadeja, had declared unilateral independence.

Hardevsinh parked the car under the branches of a lone banyan
tree on the edge of the village square. The panchayat must have
once met in the shade of that tree, but Hardevsinh pointed to a
new two-storeyed concrete building which was the parliament and
secretariat of Rajsamdhiyala. 'It's where I rule from,' he said without
a trace of modesty. A lean man, of only average height, with a
narrow foxy face and, in spite of being past fifty, a mop of black hair
which almost covered his forehead, Hardevsinh would not have
stood out in a crowd. But when you talked to him, he had the manner
and impatience of someone used to commanding obedience. As
chairman he had a large office on the ground floor of the panchayat
office building with photographs of his successful water-harvesting
on the wall – small dams holding water in previously dried-up
rivulets, and ponds which collected the rain and allowed it to
percolate through the soil to raise the groundwater level. The Indian
bureaucracy classifies these as 'minor irrigation works', as against
the major dams and canals of which they are so fond.

Two farmers from a neighbouring village were waiting for
Hardevsinh in his office. They had come to seek his help to buy
cattle fodder on concessional terms from an agricultural cooperative
of which he was a director. Unlike the sarpanch they wore traditional
Gujarati clothes, white smocks outside white cotton trousers cut
like jodhpurs, the more tight round the calves the more fashionable.
Hardevsinh rang the cooperative office in Rajkot to warn them he
would be there later in the day with the two farmers, ordered cups
of tea for us, and asked me, 'Where would you like to begin?'

'I suppose we'd better start with water, hadn't we?' I replied
rather diffidently.

'Well, the most important thing is to know where the water is.
The government has built check dams all over the place and most
of them are absolutely useless. What's even more stupid is that they
have all the information to know where they should be built.'

He opened the drawer of his desk and took out satellite images
of the underground water ducts and dykes of the area. 'Look at

these,' he instructed me. 'They have helped us to harvest water so successfully. They show where it is to be found, where it is stored underground, and where there are fractures so that it can percolate from the surface.' Pointing to thick black lines looking something like railway lines on a map he went on, 'These are the dykes, and you can see how important they are to decide where to build the dams.' I couldn't. The dykes seemed to start from nowhere and end nowhere, and I was unable to see any significance in them. So to avoid showing my ignorance I changed the subject and asked how the water was shared in the village. He explained that the panchayat ran a scheme which supplied every house with tap water and maintained public wells in addition to those owned by farmers. In return every villager paid a water tax to the panchayat.

Water isn't the only thing that is taxed in Rajsamdhiyala. The village's government is financed by a house tax, a tax for cleaning the village, and a tax on vehicles including bicycles. And raising taxes isn't the only power that the panchayat has usurped from the government. It also acts as the court and the police. Statutory fines are prescribed. Among them are fifty-one rupees for dropping litter, one hundred and fifty-one rupees for drinking alcohol, and two hundred and fifty-one rupees for gambling. Anyone found guilty of 'eve-teasing', or making a nuisance of himself with a woman, has his head shaved and is paraded through the village. If there is a theft, the panchayat immediately pays compensation to the victim and takes on the responsibility of solving the crime. No villager is allowed to approach the police; that incurs a fine of five hundred rupees.

I was a little doubtful about keeping the police away. In India they guard their turf jealously – investigating crimes and dealing with complaints is a profitable occupation. But Hardevsinh insisted, 'The police don't come here because there is no work for them to do. There are plenty of other places for them to perform their duties. There are in every place, always, some ten per cent of people who are not willing to be law-abiding but in this village we can deal with them ourselves. We have a government of our own and we are free.'

The sarpanch took considerable pleasure in telling me the fate of a gang who had robbed a farmer and a Dalit of Rajsamdhiyala six years ago. 'We managed to locate two of them, members of a nomadic caste, and we thrashed them until they told us where the others where. We broke the legs of two, and eventually we caught twenty-five altogether and dealt with them. Since then no one has dared to enter my village,' he added with a satisfied smile. Rajsamdhiyala doesn't have a written code of law. Hardevsinh despises such refinements. 'Anyone who works according to a copybook will achieve nothing. There's no appeal, no court drama here, everything is decided on the spot, the same day, and is final.'

Although the sun was by now at its height, Hardevsinh insisted on showing me round his model village. He strode, swaggered would be a slight exaggeration, along the lanes which were remarkably wide and lacking in potholes. All the houses were built of brick and plastered with concrete, only the cattle-sheds were constructed of mud.

Hardevsinh was justifiably proud of Rajsamdhiyala.

'You don't see any flies because there is no dirt and litter,' he pointed out.

'There don't seem to be any pi-dogs either,' I added.

'No,' he replied. 'We don't have any love for them.'

'You are a mini-Lee Kuan Yew,' I suggested, 'a sort of benevolent dictator with a passion for cleanliness.'

The sarpanch agreed that everything in the village was 'compulsory', but preferred to describe himself as 'a mixture of Hitler and Gandhi'.

We came across three old men, their heads shielded from the sun by white turbans, sitting on the steps of a shop. The shop was a mini-department store selling virtually anything the villagers could require. The shopkeeper had been a landless labourer but the sarpanch had organized a loan for him to start up in business.

I asked the old men whether they thought this drought really was the worst of the century.

One replied, 'We were used to hardship and living without water. Some years it was bad, some years not so bad. Some years the crops were good, some years bad, and some years there was nothing to harvest. Not so long ago, I can't remember exactly when but I think it was in the time of Rajiv Gandhi, we had three bad years together. But usually one was able to find some drinking water in the wells. This year we are told there is none.'

'Told, what do you mean?'

'We are told there is none in other villages, and there are many complaints about what the government is doing, but here we have plenty of water because of Sarpanch Sahib.'

The other old men muttered in agreement.

I asked to see the area of the village where the Dalits lived. It is usually the poorest and most neglected part of a village, but here again the houses were brick built and had little gardens. A pair of bullocks with magnificent curved horns and humps behind the yoke were harrowing a field. I was surprised, because in a prosperous north Indian village that job would be done by a tractor. But Saurashtrians are notoriously canny and Hardevsinh explained how bullocks can still be more economical than a tractor because the capital cost is very low, they require no maintenance, their fodder is cheaper than diesel, and they can reach places inaccessible to tractors.

During our discussion on the village's government, Hardevsinh had told me of a case he had dealt with only that morning. A farmer protecting his land from nilgai, members of the antelope family also known as blue bulls, had erected a fence which crossed the irrigation channel of his neighbour. A complaint had been lodged at eight o'clock and by nine o'clock Hardevsinh had persuaded the farmers to accept a compromise whereby the fence was moved and in exchange the aggrieved party surrendered some less strategic land. We went to see what the decision meant on the ground and found a labourer already digging fresh holes for the fence. The two farmers from a neighbouring village who were still patiently tagging along behind us were amazed. One said, 'In our village this dispute would have ended up in court, costing both parties a lot of money.'

'And there would have been no end to the matter, no decision,' the other added.

'That's the advantage of not having courts,' said Hardevsinh with a satisfied smile.

So far I'd seen no water, no rivulets, no streams, no ponds, and when I asked Hardevsinh about this he replied, 'You won't, the water is all underground.' He took me to see a series of concrete dams in a river bed. Each dam was about three feet high. There was no water in the river bed but peering into a nearby well I could see some water deep down in the darkness at the bottom of the shaft. There didn't appear to be much water but Hardevsinh said, 'The owner is lucky to have any water. If it wasn't for these dams what little rain we did get last year would have run away. Because it was stopped, it seeped down to the underground storage. All we need now is a single flood and in two hours the wells will be recharged and the farmer can have irrigation from this well.'

As we re-entered the main square after my tour of the village, I was somewhat distressed to see a white van parked under the banyan tree. It seemed to be done up in the livery of the Gujarat police force. Had my story collapsed, was the hero if not a liar, given to exaggeration which made his testimony unreliable? When we got nearer it became clear that the van did indeed belong to the police, but this did nothing to deflate the sarpanch's confidence. He strode into his office and greeted the two burly police officers sitting in front of the desk.

'We were just talking about the police and here you are.'

One thing did seem clear – the two policemen had waited to get permission from the sarpanch before entering the village, what was more they seemed to know him well and be on good terms. When I asked how this could be, the older of the two, a heavy jowled, pot-bellied sub-inspector from the Special Branch in Rajkot, growled, 'The panchayat here is very helpful to us. Sometimes we come here to have *chae-pani*, tea and water. But we don't have any trouble with this village.' There appeared to be a sort of Interpol relationship between the republic of Rajsamdhiyala and the Indian police. The two would exchange information and cooperate when necessary. This time the police had come to ask permission to interview a villager who had once been friendly with an absconder who had escaped from custody after being charged with adulterating petrol. Permission was granted and the police went on their way.

The poor farmers from the neighbouring village were getting a little anxious about their appointment in Rajkot, but there was still one more thing I had asked to see. Because I wasn't going to get a typical picture of the impact of the drought in Rajsamdhiyala I'd asked the sarpanch to take me to a village which had not been affected by his enthusiasm for water harvesting. So we set off in his car for the village of Padashan.

On the way, we passed yet another unusual feature of Rajsam-dhiyala, the village cricket ground with a practice match in progress. It was no lush English village green. There wasn't a blade of grass to be seen on the black sun-baked earth. We drove right up to the wicket – no player dared to object. I was relieved to see the game was being played with a tennis ball. A cricket ball would have been lethal on that hard pitch. Next to it two other pitches had been dug up and Hardevsinh assured me they would be covered with green grass by the time the season started in October. I found that difficult to believe. It was not a surprise, however, to learn that the sarpanch was captain of the village team, opening bat, and right arm leg-spin bowler.

On the way to Padashan we dropped off the two farmers from the neighbouring village, who were no nearer getting their fodder. They walked away uncomplaining after being dismissed without an apology and told to come back the next day.

As soon as we entered Padashan itself, I realized I was back in lethargic village India, its will sapped by dependence on the government, its hopes dashed by the unfulfilled promises of officials and politicians. We had difficulty in getting the car through the narrow, potholed lanes, and avoiding the mangy dogs so unloved in Rajsamdhiyala. Everywhere, it seemed, was littered with blue plastic bags. Flies buzzed around the open drains. Plaster was peeling off the wall of the temple in the centre of the village. There was no shortage of men young and old with nothing better to do than stare at us.

They gathered round us as soon as we got out of the car. Chairs were brought out and in no time at all we were in the middle of a discussion on the drought. A young man was sent to inform their sarpanch so that the diplomatic niceties could be observed. Hardevsinh was well known and highly regarded by the villagers, and no one wanted there to be any question of disrespect to him. A pot of tea appeared, but in Saurashtra it's drunk from the saucer, which to the unpractised is easier said than done. My hands trembled so much that I spilt most of the saucer's contents down my shirt.

While we were waiting for the sarpanch, I enquired about the impact of the drought. Apparently there was no water in the wells and villagers were entirely dependent on government tankers. Eight were meant to come every day, but there were the inevitable complaints about irregular supplies. Thinking of that headline about the cattle bone dealers, I asked an old farmer how many cattle had died in the village. 'I am not sure any have died,' he replied, 'but the cattle feed the government supplies is inedible so we have to pay a high price for fodder. In the big drought from '85 to '87 the government provided a cattle camp in every village.'

The *pujari*, or priest of the temple, said he could never remember a time when all the wells had been dry before. He didn't know of any cases of people becoming ill because of the water shortage, or of any migration from the village, but the village was suffering 'great hardship'. The farmers complained that although they had insured their crops with the cooperative, they hadn't been paid for last year's failure and they didn't have the money to buy seed even if the rains did come this year. I asked them why they hadn't followed the example of Rajsamdhiyala and built check dams to harvest water. The pujari replied, 'The government never did it for us.' I pointed out, 'Rajsamdhiyala has not had any help from the government.' An old farmer sitting in front of us, his hands clasped on top of his lathi, leant forward and said, 'The hand of God is not on us to have good leaders.'

At that moment the sarpanch arrived. He was a fine-looking man with neatly cut white hair and an immaculately brushed moustache, smartly turned out in trousers and a bushshirt which looked as if they had come straight off the ironing board. He had all the appearance of a man who could command authority, but when I asked him why he had not been able to organize the construction of check dams he replied, 'People here are not interested. Everyone in this village says why should we do it, the government should do it for us. The people are not helping.'

The villagers had all heard of the new scheme of the government to encourage water harvesting under which it guaranteed to fund sixty per cent of the cost of constructing dams if the village would find the remaining forty. But the old farmer clutching his stick was not impressed. 'The scheme was for ninety–ten, now it's for sixty–forty. How can we succeed?'

'He's suffering from pessimism,' Hardevsinh muttered to me, 'how can anyone do anything with that attitude.'

I asked the demoralized sarpanch what would happen if this drought lasted three years like the one in the eighties. He pointed to the heavens and said, 'The one up there knows,' and at that very moment there was a thunderous crack. But it wasn't the one up there replying, only a drummer opening the evening supplication to him in the temple by the village square. That was too much for Hardevsinh. Shrugging his shoulders in disgust he said scornfully, 'If you think doing puja to God or *sifarish* to the government is going to help you, you're mistaken. God hasn't done anything for us, nor has the government. We've done it all ourselves.'

After writing off the village, and the villagers from the sarpanch downwards, he strode off and I followed somewhat less confidently. I wasn't quite sure I wanted to be associated with the sarpanch's harsh words.

As we drove back to Rajsamdhiyala, the sun was setting behind a distant range of low hills rising abruptly from the flatlands of Saurashtra like unsightly slag-heaps. Hardevsinh noticed the banks of black clouds tinged rose pink and blood red by the last light of the sun. 'There could be rain tonight if there is a wind,' he said, and then added scornfully, 'it won't do that useless lot any good, the water will just run off their land.'

There were showers in some places that night and the next day I did see some water which had been harvested. But before that I was taken to meet one of the saints who had contributed to the water-harvesting movement. I was introduced to him by a comparatively lowly employee of the government's irrigation department who had taken leave from his job and had become the leader of a people's movement.

It was the editor of *Fulchab* who suggested I should also meet Mansukhbhai Suvagia who was credited with inspiring one hundred villages to build their own check dams in a region to the west of Rajkot. The water revolution, as Mansukhbhai called it, took off from a meeting in a village where three small dams had been built. News of this reached the chief minister of Gujarat and he agreed to attend a great assembly in the village. People came from all over Saurashtra and at the end of the proceedings they all raised their hands and took an oath to start harvesting water. Realizing that politicians' credibility was not of the highest, Mansukhbhai had also invited some fifteen saints to the meeting to add their influence to his campaign. He showed me a photograph of one elderly, and obviously much revered holy man, arriving enthroned on a tractor and accompanied by a procession of devotees. The tractor was got up like a traditional chariot with a richly embroidered parasol over the saint's head as a symbol of his dignity. Another photograph showed three saints handing over money to build dams. That, according to Mansukhbhai, who didn't share the *Fulchab* editor's high opinion of saints, was a rare sight indeed. 'This is the first time saints have given money,' he told me, 'they usually ask for money to build temples, now they are giving money for development.'

I was interested in meeting one of the water-harvesting saints, so Mansukhbhai agreed to take me to Karsan Das Bapu. We drove to the saint's headquarters and our car pulled up beside a large sandstone temple. There was no sign of any builders but bamboo scaffolding still clung precariously to the structure, and the hall, standing on a plinth, approached by some twenty steps, was as yet unoccupied by the gods. Next to the temple was a modern *dharamsala*, or rest house, for pilgrims and other visitors. On the opposite side of the spacious compound, lined with palm trees, was a long, low shed with a red corrugated iron roof. This turned out to be the dining hall. Sitting on the ground (the dining hall had no floor), we were served watery vegetable curry and even more watery daal, the standard fare in Indian religious establishments. Then we retired to bedrooms in the rest house and waited for the saint to receive us. As the time passed I became worried because I didn't want to miss a public meeting Mansukhbhai had scheduled for five o'clock, but Mansukhbhai didn't share my concern.

At last, we were shown into the saint's chamber, and seated below his throne, which was a bed rather than a chair. I was expecting a regal figure, someone demanding and accustomed to reverence, but eventually a slight, wizened man, clad inevitably in saffron robes, with thinning, oiled hair plastered over his skull, slipped into the room, went straight up to Mansukhbhai, embraced him, pinched his cheek and asked, 'How are you my friend?'

Karsan Das Bapu may have been a holy man but that didn't stop him having a sense of humour. When I asked him about the temple he was building he laughed, 'I suppose this young man has been telling you I am a beggar who takes money to build temples when what we need is dams.'

'Well, not exactly,' I replied. 'He did say saints used to do that but he also showed me a picture of some saints giving him money for dams.'

'Was I one of them?'

I didn't think so, but I didn't want to embarrass Mansukhbhai. Fortunately he spotted the trap before I could put my foot in it, and intervened, 'I knew you wouldn't expect any reward or any acknowledgement for your generosity. After all it says in the *Gita* that you should do your duty with no thought for the consequences.'

'Of course you are right,' chuckled the saint, leaning forward to pinch Mansukhbhai's cheek again. 'When we first met I told you that you were doing what we saints do, social service, but without wearing our robes. Now it seems you want to take over my job of teaching dharma too. Have you also told this man what I taught you – that God is everywhere including in water. Water is H_2O and God is the hydrogen in water?'

After Mansukhbhai assured him that he had not been teaching

me the theology of water, the saint went on to explain that if God was the hydrogen in water obviously we should not waste it, so it was our dharmic duty to harvest it.

The saint admitted he had needed convincing before he was converted to water harvesting. 'Local officials,' he said, 'told me it was all a waste of time and all that was needed was to complete the dam on the River Narmada, which they said would bring water to Saurashtra. But then I agreed to meet Mansukhbhai and I could see he was a good boy. So I went to see his work and realized that it was just jealousy speaking against him, so I gave him money.'

'What do you mean by jealousy, who was jealous?' I asked.

'In India no one likes to see anyone going ahead. They will always try to pull him down, especially if they are politicians who know they are unpopular and so fear popular leaders like Mansukhbhai.'

When we stood up to leave, the saint pinched my cheek and gave me an unusual blessing, 'Now you are my friend too. Of course, I don't know whether you are a good boy also, but I'm sure you will be now with Mansukhbhai to guide you.'

Now at last we were to see water. We drove past mile after mile of flat fields, their rich black soil prepared for the groundnut and cotton seeds which would only be sown if and when the monsoon came. There was no grass. The only vegetation was stunted, scrawny trees, scrub, and cactus. Last night's monsoon showers had bequeathed a few puddles which had not yet been dried out by the fierce summer sun. At last we came to a small village where we were greeted enthusiastically by the local doctor. Accompanied by half the village, he took us to what had been a dry river bed and there we saw black crows gulping water greedily and cows drinking contentedly from a pond which had built up behind one of Mansu-khbhai's check dams. The doctor admitted, 'We were all doubtful about this scheme because we had forgotten the tradition of harvesting rain. Now we can see with our own eyes that it works. This water will take a long time to evaporate and all the time it's seeping underground too.'

By now we were more than two hours late for the meeting Mansukhbhai was due to address at the village of Bhalgam. When we did eventually arrive, a worried social worker, Madhibhai Vekaria, was waiting for us on the outskirts but he didn't receive an apology for the anxiety and inconvenience we had caused him. That didn't seem to worry him; he was just relieved that we had turned up in the end. As we drove through the village he leant out of the car window shouting, 'Mansukhbhai has come, the meeting will start now. The BBC man has come, the meeting will start now.' I didn't want to undermine his efforts to drum up a crowd by pointing out that I was longer a BBC man.

Villagers rose from the tea shop and from other stalls, from doorsteps and from the shade of trees, from all the places where they had gathered in small knots for the evening review of events local and national. They made their way to the barren land outside the village, the meeting ground. We went ahead of them to find that some people were already waiting patiently for us.

There was a wind that evening and so the social worker's introduction was interrupted by the microphone squawking and screeching. Various attempts to solve that problem by tying handkerchiefs round the microphone were eventually successful and by the time Mansukhbhai came to speak he could be heard loud and clear as he declaimed, 'For the last two hundred years you have bowed down under all your difficulties thinking whatever they are God will solve them. You have forgotten your own responsibilities and become lazy. I want this laziness to end and I want you to solve your own problems.'

Mansukhbhai spoke ad lib, never pausing to search for a word. Young, not particularly tall, and dressed in a long-sleeved white shirt tucked into his trousers with the obligatory ballpoint pen in the top pocket he looked like any other junior government clerk. Yet the village elders sitting in front of him, and their sons behind them, took this criticism without a murmur.

'I believe in God,' Mansukhbhai went on, 'but I don't want to unload all my troubles on to Him. I don't have faith in the government, so it's useless to unload your troubles on them. I have seen the power of the people. If you take that power into your hands you will see what you can achieve.'

It was difficult to tell from the phlegmatic faces of the villagers whether the message had hit home. But after the meeting, at a gathering of village notables in a house which surprised me with its opulence, I was assured it had.

No story in India is complete without allegations of corruption and water harvesting was no exception. According to Mansukhbhai it was because the chief minister of Gujarat was so moved by the meeting he'd attended that he had promised the government would finance sixty per cent of any water harvesting scheme if the villagers themselves put up the remaining forty per cent. He'd done this in spite of the fact that Gujarati politicians of all parties were totally committed to the theory that the Narmada dam was the one and only answer to Saurashtra's water problems. Not everyone agrees with Mansukhbhai's version of the origins of the chief minister's scheme, but nobody, not even officials, denied it had spawned corruption, especially in the district of Junagadh. There, according to press reports, the government had stopped handing out money because there was so much corruption.

Junagadh is about one hundred kilometres from Rajkot. On the way there I passed a small group of Jain nuns, recognizable by their thin white cotton robes. One nun, enthroned in a cumbersome wooden wheelchair, was being pushed by a lay woman. The rest were walking barefoot on a murderous Indian main road which made no concessions to pedestrians. I hesitated to stop and talk to the nuns for fear they would consider that an intrusion, but in the end I couldn't resist the temptation to satisfy my curiosity. I told the driver to turn the car round and go back to them. To my surprise the first nun I approached was quite willing to talk to me. She spoke softly and her speech was muffled by a white cloth tied across her mouth to prevent her accidentally swallowing even the smallest insect and thereby breaching the Jain code of absolute respect for all life, and so I didn't catch all she said. I did gather that the group was on a pilgrimage to Veraval on the coast which would mean two months on the road in the heat of summer and the humidity of the monsoon. That day they planned to reach a village about nine kilometres away. All the nuns carried their meagre possessions wrapped up in a white cloth and something like a floor-mop to sweep away the insects from the ground in front of them. I asked if I could take a photograph and that was politely refused.

I'd always wanted to go to Junagadh because of the fascinating story of the flight of its ruler shortly after India became independent. Under the British, Saurashtra was a patchwork of princely states, they varied from Junagadh with a population of 608,000 and more than three thousand square miles in area to tiny states like Manavadar, whose Khan only ruled over one hundred square miles. Junagadh was the only major Saurashtrian state to be ruled by a Muslim, Nawab Sahib Sir Mahbatkhan Rasulkhanji. He was a ruler who took more interest in his dogs than his subjects, once declaring a public holiday to celebrate the wedding of two of his favourite canine companions. Not being a very decisive ruler, he easily fell under the influence of his *dewan*, or chief minister, Sir Shah Nawaz Bhutto. He, like his son, Zulfikar Ali Bhutto, the executed Prime Minister of Pakistan, had a penchant for plotting. Sir Shah Nawaz's scheme was to get the Nawab to declare that his state would opt to join Muslim Pakistan even though some eighty per cent of his subjects were Hindus. The other major states of Saurashtra had opted the other way which meant he would have been surrounded on all sides either by India or the sea. The Nawab fell for the scheme but lost his nerve and fled when food ran short because neighbouring states refused to trade with him, his subjects became restive, and the Indian army camped on his border. He was in such a hurry that he forgot one of his wives but many of his dogs did manage to board the flight.

The Nawab left behind a city that had been a capital many centuries before his forefathers established their dynasty in the 1730s. The town was built on the plains in the shadow of the hill of Girnar, which had been sacred to Jains for centuries. The hill was studded with temples and the town's long history was marked by many monuments, including Buddhist caves maybe fifteen hundred years old, an ancient fort with a mosque for Friday prayers within its walls, and the mausoleums of the Nawab's own dynasty, each with its own minarets. Most of the monuments remain, but what must have been a colourful small town has been overrun by modern India with its unsightly development so unplanned that the drains in the streets I was driving through couldn't cope with a mere monsoon shower.

I came eventually to a government guest house where, through the good offices of a journalist from Ahmedabad, I was to meet some young party workers from the Bharatiya Janata Party, which was in power in Gujarat and in Delhi. They, I'd been told, had evidence of corruption in the sixty–forty scheme. I found them in the guest house's VVIP bedroom where they were complaining to the local MP, herself from the BJP, that during a recent spot check of nine dams built under the scheme, eight were found to be 'of inferior quality'. The MP was told there was no problem when dams were built by villagers themselves, the problem arose when contractors were brought in.

The workers were surprisingly willing to talk about their own government's corruption to me, although I was a journalist, and deputed Nirbhai Purohit, the young general secretary of the Juna-gadh BJP, to take me to the site of a dam constructed by a contractor. We drove to the small town of Mendarda where we picked up Mohanbhai, the local secretary of the BJP, a disagreeable looking man, with receding hair brightly coloured by henna. He was reluctant to part with any information beyond the instructions necessary to find our way to the dam. After driving several miles through increasingly desolate countryside, he told the driver to turn off the tarmac road down a bumpy track. There was no sign of civilization or cultivation, not a tree in sight. Suddenly, in the middle of this rock-strewn, barren wilderness, our guide pointed to some figures in the distance, and mumbled, 'That's the dam site.'

Drawing nearer we could see that, as so often happens in India, the hard work was being done by women. Brightly coloured skirts swirling round their ankles, hips swaying, shoulders shifting to balance the metal pans on their heads, they strode confidently across the uneven terrain, miraculously not tripping over their wholly unsuitable sandals. They were a human conveyor belt filling a cement mixer with earth and stone and carrying the resultant unstable compound to the dam site. The dam was almost complete and a young man was busy disguising the true nature of its construction by plastering a thin layer of concrete over the earth and stone embankment. The surly, unshaven supervisor denied all responsibility for the fraud that was being perpetuated. He only did what the contractor told him to do.

'Anyhow,' he asked, 'how do you know this is meant to be a cement dam? The government inspectors came here two days ago and passed it as ninety per cent all right.'

But Mohanbhai knew the contract was for a cement dam.

On the way back Mohanbhai opened up when asked how the scam worked. 'Any eleven people can get together and form a committee to build a dam,' he explained. 'They don't have to be a village panchayat or any recognized body. Officials are too anxious to give the money away.'

'Why?' I asked.

Mohanbhai looked at me as if I was an idiot. 'Because they get a share of it of course. No one checks the dam site, no one checks the estimate, no one checks the dam when it's built. There have been reports of some dams which haven't even been built and yet the contractors get a completion certificate. Money is flowing into the officials' pockets.'

'So how does it work when villagers build dams?'

'That's a different matter. First of all, the committee is not a fraud, then the villagers themselves do the work and watch it to see there is no cheating. After all, they are interested in saving water not making money.'

Before coming to Rajkot I had met the minister for information in Ahmedabad and he'd explained the efforts the government had made to eradicate corruption in the sixty–forty scheme, and other drought relief measures. The drought-stricken areas had been divided into five zones and teams of inspectors had been sent to each one. 'It wasn't just a case of set a thief to catch a thief,' the minister had said. 'In each team there was a member of the chamber of commerce as well as a senior official, an engineer, and a member of the state assembly.

I asked Mohanbhai whether this was all eyewash.

Before he could answer, the Junagadh BJP secretary butted in, 'No. You heard me tell the MP that the teams had come, but much of the damage had been done by then.'

'So if the teams are so effective why have we just seen an obvious example of corruption still going on?'

'Well, you can't plug every leak of government money, but we have reported this and Mohanbhai will see they don't get a completion certificate.'

'I will most certainly,' said Mohanbhai grimly.

I had to get the official version of the dam scandal, and so I sought an appointment with the civil servant who had been sent to Saurashtra as special relief commissioner. He willingly agreed to see me in his official bungalow opposite what was once Rajkot's race-course and is now a rather indeterminate open space. I was shown into the sitting room by a servant to wait for the commissioner, but I didn't have to wait long before a small stout man, of an owlish academic appearance, hurried into the room and introduced himself as Pravin Trivedi. He had been posted in Rajkot earlier and everyone described him as 'a clean officer'.

The commissioner blamed misuse of technology in part for the crisis. In the last drought submersible pumps were not available, now the commissioner said they were playing havoc with the water table. They were pumping water from depths of a thousand feet or more, which could only be described as 'water mining'. Ironically Mansukhbhai, the leader of the water-harvesting movement, was able to take leave from the government because of the generosity of his brother who manufactured submersible pumps.

Pravin Trivedi was an enthusiast for the people's movement. Whereas most bureaucrats resent anything that takes power out of their hands, he was all in favour of giving as much freedom as possible to the villagers. 'That's the best part of the scheme,' he said. 'It gives the villagers the responsibility to design and build the dams. It is essential to use the engineering skills of the people. After all, they used to harvest water for centuries without the help of any government.'

'What about the corruption then, what causes that?'

'Corruption? I don't want to magnify it. This is an excellent scheme and it must not be spoilt by unsubstantiated allegations of corruption which you always get with government work.'

'So there is no corruption?'

'No, of course I can't say that. When such a vast movement comes into being there will be irregularities but we must not blame the entire scheme. It really works. The villagers don't just build dams with their labour, they put their souls into them. You must not undermine them by believing exaggerations about corruption.'

'So, why then,' I asked, 'has the scheme been cancelled in Junagadh?'

The commissioner played that back effortlessly, 'It hasn't been actually cancelled in Junagadh or any other district.'

As I was bringing our conversation to an end the commissioner realized that he might have allowed his enthusiasm to run away with him. Remembering that the official line was to rubbish water harvesting in case it detracted from the case for completing the Narmada dam he said anxiously, 'Please don't think that anything I have said can be interpreted as meaning that we don't need the Narmada dam. We must have that water if we are to have an adequate supply because harvesting alone can never fulfil all Saurashtra's needs.'

The Gujarat government had appointed a special minister for the Narmada and he had published a very effective counterblast to his opponents. Reading through it, I had come to realize that there were arguments in favour of the dam, just as there were arguments against it. But the minister had spoilt his argument by falling into the trap of the false alternative, the either-or argument. In stressing the need for Narmada he'd written off water harvesting. In one particular instance he had been manifestly wrong. Unable to ignore the renown of the sarpanch of Rajsamdhiyala which had spread far and wide, he'd stated in his document 'the success of Rajsamdhiyala is due to typical topographical and geological features . . . the same could not be replicated even in the nearby vicinity due to non-availability of such geological advantage.' But I had seen another success with my own eyes.

On my last day in Saurashtra I took this document to the formidable sarpanch. He was enraged and, ignoring my protests that I didn't understand the satellite maps, insisted on coming back to Rajkot with me to photocopy them so that I could have some scientific evidence with me to refute the minister's claim.

After photocopying the maps Hardevsinh took me to lunch in one of Rajkot's smartest restaurants. During the meal he told me a minister had once attacked him as an enemy of his motherland because he'd criticized Narmada.

'So what do you think about it now?' I asked.

'Well, I'm not sure.'

'That doesn't seem very like you.'

The sarpanch laughed and then fell silent, which was also unusual, before saying, 'I don't see why we shouldn't have both – water harvesting and Narmada. Certainly if we have Narmada that doesn't mean we should waste water.'

That surely is true. The dispute over Narmada will continue long after the court's decision. What can't be disputed here and now is that the way the dam has dominated the water policy of western India is all too typical of India's longstanding policy of seeking large-scale solutions to problems and ignoring the contribution small-scale schemes can also make. Himanshu Thakkar of the South Asian Network on Dams, Rivers and People is an opponent of Narmada, but that doesn't invalidate his description of India's water policy as 'top down, engineer-bureaucrat-politician-contractor driven, dominated by large projects and structures'. But most important of all, according to the NGO leader, is that, 'There is no role for the people.' Hardevsinh and other leaders of the water harvesting movement have forced the government of Gujarat to concede them a role. They have been faithful to the Mahatma who once said, 'I heartily endorse the proposition that any plan which

"We must make our choice. We may have democracy, or we may have wealth concentrated in the hands of a few, but we can't have both."
—Louis Brandeis

"The crisis consists precisely in the fact that the old is dying and the new cannot be born; in this interregnum a great variety of morbid symptoms appear."
—Antonio Gramsci

"Strategic inflection points . . . can mean an opportunity to rise to new heights. But it may just as likely signal the beginning of the end."
—Andy Grove

CONTENTS

PART FOUR | Same Old Same Old

PART FIVE | Make America New Again

INTRODUCTION

When you reach your fifties, it gets easier to notice the big ways in which the world has or hasn't changed since you were young, both the look and feel of things and people's understandings of how society works. A half-century of life is enough to provide some panoramic perspective, letting you see and sense arcs of history firsthand, like when an airplane reaches the altitude where the curvature of the Earth becomes visible.

Some of the arcs of historical change are obvious, their paths as well as their causes. The equality and empowerment of women is one of those big *duh* ones. But other important historical arcs, more complicated or obscure, have to be figured out.

That's how I came to write my last nonfiction book, a not-so-obvious American history called *Fantasyland: How America Went Haywire*. I'd noticed that in so many ways, as Stephen Colbert joked on the first episode of his old nightly show, America had become increasingly "divided between those who think with their head and those who *know* with their *heart*." From the 1960s and '70s on, I realized, America had really changed in this regard. Belief in every sort of make-believe had spun out of control—in religion, science, politics, and lifestyle, all of them merging with entertainment in what I called the fantasy-industrial complex. In that book I explained the deep, centuries-long history of this American knack for creating and believing the excitingly untrue. As soon as I finished writing *Fantasyland*, we elected a president who was its single most florid and consequential expression ever, a poster boy embodying all its themes.

But that long-standing, chronic American condition that turned into an acute crisis is just half the story of how and why we've come to grief these last few decades. This other part concerns the transformation of our social system that started in the 1970s and '80s, helped along by a simultaneous plunge into compulsive nostalgia and wariness of the new and unfamiliar. Whereas *Fantasyland* concerned Americans' centuries-old weakness for the untrue and irrational, and its spontaneous and dangerous flowering since the 1960s, *Evil Geniuses* chronicles the quite deliberate reengineering of our economy and society since the 1960s by a highly rational confederacy of the rich, the right, and big business.

From my parents' young adulthood in the 1930s and '40s through my young adulthood in the 1970s, American economic life became a lot more fair and democratic and secure than it had been when my parents were children in the 1920s and early '30s. But then all of a sudden around 1980, that progress slowed, stopped, and in many ways reversed.

I didn't start fully appreciating and understanding the nature and enormity of that change until the turn of this century, after the country had been transformed. In 2002, when several spectacular corporate financial frauds were exposed and their CEO perpetrators prosecuted, I published a long screed in *The New York Times* blaming Wall Street. "If infectious greed is the virus, New York is the center of the outbreak," I wrote, because it

> is also, inarguably, the money center of America and the world, the capital of capitalism. . . . It was New York investment bankers who drove the mergers-and-acquisitions deal culture of the 80's and 90's and who most aggressively oversold the myth of synergy that justified it. . . . It was they . . . who invented the novel financial architectures of Enron and WorldCom. It was the example of New York investment bankers, earning gigantic salaries for doing essentially nothing—knowing the right people, talking smoothly, showing up at closings—that encouraged businesspeople out in the rest of America to feel entitled to smoke-and-mirrors cash bonanzas of their own.

A few years later, one very cold morning just after Thanksgiving, I had another slow-road-to-Damascus moment from whatever I had been (complacent neoliberal?) to whatever I was becoming (appalled social democrat?). I was actually on the road to Eppley Airfield in Omaha after my first visit to my hometown since both my parents had died, sharing a minivan jitney from a hotel with a couple of Central Casting airline pilots—tall, fit white men around my age, one wearing a leather jacket. We chatted. To my surprise, even shock, both of them spent the entire trip sputtering and whining—about being baited and switched when their employee ownership shares of United Airlines had been evaporated by its recent bankruptcy, about the default of their pension plan, about their CEO's recent 40 percent pay raise, about the company to which they'd devoted their entire careers but no longer trusted at all. In effect, about changing overnight from successful all-American middle-class professionals who'd worked hard and played by the rules into disrespected, cheated, sputtering, whining chumps.

When we got to the airport, I said goodbye and good luck and, at the little bookstore there that contains a kind of shrine to the local god Warren Buffett and his company Berkshire Hathaway, bought a newspaper. In it I read an article about that year's record-setting bonuses on Wall Street. The annual revenues of Goldman Sachs were greater than the annual economic output of two-thirds of the countries on Earth—a treasure chest from which the firm was disbursing the equivalent of $69 million to its CEO and an average of $800,000 apiece to *everybody else* at the place.*

This was 2006, before Wall Street started teetering, before the financial crash, before the Great Recession. The amazing real estate bubble had not yet popped, and the economy was still apparently rocking.

I was writing a regular column for *New York* magazine, so after reading and thinking some more, I summarized my understanding of how an egregiously revised American social contract had been put in place, take it or leave it, without much real debate.

"This is not the America in which we grew up," I wrote.

By which I meant America of the several very prosperous decades

*Historical sums of money are pretty meaningless because of inflation—$1,000 in 2020 is the same as $850 in 2010, $500 in 1990, $150 in 1970, and so on. So throughout this book, unless I specify otherwise, all dollar amounts are inflation-adjusted, even when I don't mention that I've rendered a historical sum in "today's dollars" or that it was "equivalent to" the larger present-day amount.

after World War II, when "the income share of the superrich was reasonably cut back, by more than half. The rich were still plenty rich, and
American capitalism worked fine." I wrote about how, since the 1980s,
"the piece of the income pie taken each year by the rich has become as
hugely disproportionate as it was in the 1920s," how "an average CEO
now gets paid several hundred times the salary of his average worker,
a gap that's an order of magnitude larger than it was in the 1970s," and
how most Americans' wages had barely budged. I wrote that "during the
past two decades we've not only let economic uncertainty and unfairness
grow to grotesque extremes, we've also inured ourselves to the spectacle."
By *we* I meant the mostly liberal, mostly affluent New Yorkers and other
cosmopolites who read *New York*.

After this twenty-five-year "run of pedal-to-the-metal hypercapital-
ism," I wrote, it was "now time to ease up and share the wealth some.
Because the future that frightens me isn't so much a too-Hispanic U.S.
caused by unchecked Mexican immigration, but a Latin Americanized
society with a . . . callous oligarchy gated off from a growing mass of
screwed-over peons." We needed to take seriously the rising anger and
disgust about an American economic system that seems more and more
rigged in favor of the extremely fortunate.

> Populism has gotten a bad odor, and not just among plutocrats—
> for most of the political chattering class, it is at least faintly pejo-
> rative. But I think that's about to change: When economic hope
> shrivels and the rich become cartoons of swinish privilege, why
> shouldn't the middle class become populists?

I remember thinking, *This* was why my professors in college had
used the terms *political economics* and *the political economy* as distinct
from simply *economics* and *the economy*. For one thing, *economics* has the
connotation of pure science, suggesting that organizing production and
pay and investment and taxes and all the rest is just . . . math. Whereas
political economics contains the crucial reminder that real-life societies
and economies are the result of all kinds of fights and negotiations and
feelings and choices about the rules of the game, what's fair, what's not,
what to maximize, how to optimize for the majority instead of maximizing
only for some powerful minority. It's fine to call it *the economy* when we're

discussing what's happening month to month or year to year—the ups and downs in the stock market and rates of employment and inflation and growth. Whereas if we're talking about the whole megillah, the way we've structured our capitalism versus the versions in Canada or Denmark or Russia or China, I think *political economy* is much better. The economy is weather, the political economy is climate.

I also thought: *Mea culpa*. For those last two decades, I'd prospered and thrived in the new political economy. And unhurt by automation or globalization or the new social contract, I'd effectively ignored the fact that the majority of my fellow Americans weren't prospering or thriving.

I seldom have epiphanies, but a few months later, in 2007, I happened to have another, this one concerning the culture, and it would eventually cross-fertilize with my new sense of the hijacked, screwed-up political economy. This second aha moment started with an observation I had one morning concerning personal style. Looking at a photo in the newspaper taken twenty years earlier of a large group of very stylish people on a U.S. city street, I closely examined the way each of them looked, their clothes and hair and makeup. They were virtually indistinguishable from people of the present day. I thought about that, conducted some research, and realized it was a broad phenomenon, true throughout the culture— music, design, cars, more. Apart from cellphones and computers, almost nothing anymore that was new or just a bit old looked or sounded either distinctly new or distinctly old.

This was not only not the America in which I'd grown up, when the look and feel of things changed a lot every decade or so, *it wasn't the way things had worked in the modern age, for a century or two.* In the past, certainly in my lifetime and that of my parents and grandparents, over any given twenty-year period, whenever you glanced back, you'd notice how culture and what was deemed current changed unmistakably from top to bottom. Since the dawn of the modern, ordinary people could date cultural artifacts and ephemera of the recent past and previous eras. During the twentieth century, each *decade* had its own signature look and feel. By the late 1960s, the 1950s looked *so '50s*, and by the early 1980s, the 1960s looked *so '60s*. But then, starting in the 1990s, that unstoppable flow of modernity—the distinctly *new* continuously appearing and making styles seem old—somehow slowed and nearly stopped. The dramatic new change in the culture seemed to be that things were no longer dramatically changing.

How strange.

And *why*? The shortest and simplest answer is that a massive counter-reaction to multiple overwhelming waves of newness on multiple fronts, one after another, sent all sorts of Americans, for all sorts of different reasons, to seek the reassurance of familiarity and continuity wherever they could manage to find or fake it.

The first wave was in the 1960s, a decade in which *everything* seemed relentlessly new new *new*. Which for several years felt exciting and *good* to most Americans, and the novelty glut seemed under control by the forces of reason and order. But then came the upheavals of the second half of the 1960s, when society and culture changed startlingly in just a few dozen months. In the early 1970s, exhausted by that flux, still processing the discombobulating changes concerning gender and race and sex and other norms, people all at once started looking fondly back in time at the real and imaginary good old days. Enough with the constant shocks of the new! Hollywood revived and celebrated the recent past in a big way, right away, with nostalgia-fests like *American Graffiti, Happy Days,* and *Grease.* Soon nostalgia for *all* periods kicked in throughout all media and all cultural forms with a breadth and depth that were unprecedented in America.

As people gave themselves over to finding and fondling quaint things that had been stored away in the national attic during the century of novelty and progress, we inevitably amended our view of the entire American past, romanticizing and idealizing it, tending to ignore the bad parts. As it turned out, curating and then *reproducing* pieces of the past extended beyond pop culture and style into politics and the economy. I'm not saying the freshly nostalgia-swamped culture of the 1970s and '80s *caused* people to become more politically conservative. But it wasn't a coincidence that the two phenomena emerged simultaneously. They operated in tandem. The political right rode in on that floodtide of nostalgia, and then, ironically, the old-time every-man-for-himself political economy they reinstalled, less fair and less secure, drove people deeper into their various nostalgic havens for solace. This new fixation of the culture on the old and the familiar didn't subside. It became a fixed backward gaze. Then almost without a pause came another wave of disruption and uncertainty, caused by the digital technologies that revolutionized the ways people earned livings and lived, and which made economic life for most people even more insecure. And the culture in turn focused even more compulsively on recycling and rebooting familiar styles and fashions and music and movies and shows.

Then we moved onto the weird next stage, the latest stage that I first noticed in the 2000s, after my double-take at that old photo—the *stasis:* in addition to letting the past charm us, in the 1990s we also stopped creating the fundamentally, strikingly new, perfecting a comfortable *Matrix* illusion that in some sense the world wasn't really changing all that much.

As I was working on *Fantasyland,* reading and thinking about American history, I noticed more connections between the two phenomena— between our simultaneous switch in the 1970s and '80s to a grisly old-fashioned political economy *and* to a strenuously, continuously familiar culture. Which led me to spend a couple of years reading and thinking more deeply about both.

A *lot* more deeply about the economics and politics. That's what I'd mainly studied in college, but since then I'd mostly just read the news, skimmed along day to day and month to month like anybody whose job never required knowing a lot about deregulation, antitrust, tax codes, pensions, the healthcare industry, the legal fraternity, constitutional law, organized labor, executive compensation, lobbying, billionaires' networks, the right wing, the dynamics of economic growth, stock buybacks, the financial industry and all its innovations—so many subjects of which I was mostly ignorant.

My immersion was revelatory. Reading hundreds of books and scholarly papers and articles and having conversations with experts made me more or less fluent in those subjects and, more, taught me many small things and one important big thing: what happened around 1980 and afterward was larger and uglier and more multifaceted than I'd known. *Inequality* is the buzzword, mainly because that's so simple and quantifiable: in forty years, the share of wealth owned by our richest 1 percent has doubled, the collective net worth of the bottom half has dropped almost to zero, the median weekly pay for a full-time worker has increased by just 0.1 percent a year, *only* the incomes of the top 10 percent have grown in sync with the economy, and so on. Americans' boats stopped rising together; most of the boats stopped rising at all. But along with economic *inequality* reverting to the levels of a century ago and earlier, so has economic *insecurity,* as well as the corrupting political power of big business and the rich, *oligarchy,* while economic *immobility* is almost certainly worse than it's ever been.

Before I started my research, I'd understood the changes in the 1970s and '80s hadn't all just . . . *happened,* spontaneously. But I didn't know how long and concerted and strategic the project by the political right and the rich and big business had been. One of my subjects in *Fantasyland* is how conspiracy-theorizing became an American bad habit, a way our chronic mixing of fiction and reality got the best of us. Of course there are secretive cabals of powerful people who work to make big bad things happen, actual conspiracies, but the proliferation of conspiracy *theories* since the 1960s, so many so preposterous, had the unfortunate effect of making reasonable people ignore real plots in plain sight. Likewise, the good reflex to search for and focus on the complexities and nuances of any story, on grays rather than simple whites and blacks, can tend to blind us to some plain dark truths.

I still insist on a preponderance of evidence before I draw conclusions. I still resist reducing messy political and economic reality to catchphrases like "vast right-wing conspiracy" and "the system is rigged," but I discovered that in this case the blunt shorthand is essentially correct. It looks more like arson than a purely accidental fire, more like poisoning than a completely natural illness, more like a cheating of the many by the few. After all, as the god of the economic right himself, Adam Smith, wrote in capitalism's 1776 bible, *The Wealth of Nations:* "People of the same trade seldom meet together, even for merriment and diversion, but the conversation ends in a conspiracy against the public, or in some contrivance to raise prices."

Evil Geniuses is the book I wish had existed a dozen years ago to help clarify and organize and deepen and focus my thinking and understanding and anger and blame. Like most people over the past decade, I'd noticed this fact here or that infographic there about inequality or insecurity or malign corporate power, but quickly moved on, flittered off to the next headline. But then I decided to go deep into the weeds in order to understand, then come out of the weeds to explain what I'd learned as clearly as I could. I wanted to distill and gather and connect the important facts and explanations in one compact package, to make a coherent picture out of all the puzzle pieces. There are lots of facts and figures in here, but not much jargon at all. By chronicling CEOs and billionaires and intellectuals and zealots and operators planning and strategizing for years, together and apart, networking and plotting, even memorializing some plots in memos—so many jaw-dropping *memos*—I've tried to tell a compelling story as well as make a persuasive argument about what's become of us.

So how did big business and the very rich and their political allies and enablers manage to convince enough Americans in the 1970s and '80s that the comfortable economic rules and expectations we'd had in place for half of the twentieth century were obsolete and should be replaced by an older set of assumptions and protocols?

Most people at the time didn't realize just how immense and pervasive the changes were and certainly not where they'd lead. Reagan's election and landslide reelection were plainly big deals, *some* sort of national mandate, but at the time the 1980s seemed more like a post-1960s reversion to the historically typical, not really its own moment of wrenching transformation. Whereas during the 1960s, everyone was aware we were experiencing a great turning point in culture and politics, with almost everything changing in obvious ways—like how in the '30s people were aware in real time that the Depression and New Deal were transformative, the beginning of a new America. The specific policy changes in the 1980s were profound in the aggregate, but beyond the nostalgic Reaganite Morning in America and freer-free-markets messaging, most of the changes were complicated and esoteric and seemed small, so they had a stealth quality. It didn't feel quite like a paradigm shift because it was mainly carried out by means of a thousand wonky adjustments to government rules and laws, and obscure financial inventions, and big companies one by one changing how they operated and getting away with it—all of it with impacts that emerged gradually, over decades. Social Security and Medicare benefits were not cut, the EPA wasn't abolished, labor unions weren't banned. As it turned out, the 1980s were the '30s but in reverse: instead of a fast-acting New Deal, a time-release Raw Deal.

But the reengineering was helped along because the masterminds of the economic right brilliantly used the madly proliferating nostalgia. By dressing up their mean new rich-get-richer system in old-time patriotic drag. By portraying low taxes on the rich and unregulated business and weak unions and a weak federal government as the only ways back to some kind of rugged, frontiersy, stronger, *better* America. And by choosing as their front man a winsome 1950s actor in a cowboy hat, the very embodiment of a certain flavor of American nostalgia.

Of course, Ronald Reagan didn't cheerfully *announce* in 1980 that if Americans elected him, private profit and market values would override all other American values; that as the economy grew nobody but the well-to-do would share in the additional bounty; that many millions of middle-class jobs and careers would vanish, along with fixed private pensions and reliable healthcare; that a college degree would simultaneously become unaffordable and almost essential to earning a good income; that enforcement of antimonopoly laws would end; that meaningful control of political contributions by big business and the rich would be declared unconstitutional; that Washington lobbying would increase by 1,000 percent; that our revived and practically religious deference to business would enable a bizarre American denial of climate science and absolute refusal to treat the climate crisis as a crisis; that after doubling the share of the nation's income that it took for itself, a deregulated Wall Street would nearly bring down the financial system, ravage the economy, and pay no price for its recklessness; and that the federal government he'd committed to discrediting and undermining would thus be especially ill-equipped to deal with a pandemic and its consequences.

Rather, when we were promised in 1980 the wonderful old-fashioned life of Bedford Falls, we didn't pay close enough attention to the fine print and possible downsides, and forty years later here we are in Pottersville instead, living in the world actually realized by Reaganism, our political economy remade by big business and the wealthy to maximize the wealth and power of big business and the well-to-do at the expense of everyone else. We were hoodwinked, *and* we hoodwinked ourselves.

Our wholesale national plunge into nostalgia in the 1970s and afterward was an important part of how we got on the road toward extreme insecurity and inequality, to American economic life more like the era of plutocrats and robber barons of the 1870s. All our clocks got turned back—the political and economic ones by design, the cultural ones more or less spontaneously. Economic progress ended, and cultural innovation stagnated except in information technology, where unchecked new industrial giants arose—resembling those of that first Gilded Age. The morphing of the nostalgia addiction into cultural paralysis in the 1990s helped to keep us shackled in an unpleasant perpetual present ever since. That cultural stasis, almost everyone and everything looking and sounding more or less the way they did a generation ago, provided daily reinforcement of the sense that the status quo is permanent and unchangeable across the board—in other words, a kind of fatalistic hopelessness of the kind that was standard before democracy existed, before revolutions, before the Enlightenment. We've thus been discouraged by the culture as well as by much of politics from imagining that the economy might be radically redesigned and remade once *again,* encouraged to think that fundamental change is either no longer possible or no longer desirable or both. If the present is more or less indistinguishable from the recent past, why won't the future be pretty much the same as the present but with more robots? There are the gadgets and bits of fresh software, but otherwise we have become unaccustomed to the new, many of us skeptical and afraid of the new, confused about how to think of the past or cope with the future.

Unlike longing for a fairer economy of the kind we used to have, which would require a *collective* decision to bring back, the itch of cultural and social nostalgia is easy for *individuals* to scratch and keep scratching. So for many Americans, who spent several decades losing their taste for the culturally new and/or getting screwed by a new political economy based on new technology, fantasies about restoring the past have turned pathological. Thus the angriest organized resistance to the new, the nostalgias driving the upsurge of racism and sexism and nativism—which gave us a president who seemed excitingly new because he asserted an impossible dream of restoring the nastily, brutishly old. The recent wave of politicized nostalgia is global, of course, taking over governments from Britain to Russia to India. But those countries at least have the excuse of being ancient.

"We respect the past," President Obama said of Americans when I was just beginning work on this book, right before he was replaced by President Trump, "but we don't *pine* for it. We don't fear the future; we grab for it. We are boisterous and diverse and full of energy, perpetually young in spirit." As was his wont, he was being aspirational, wishful, reminding us of our better angels. It was his gentle, upbeat way of saying hey, you know, folks, we really *have* been obsessively pining for the past and excessively fearing the future.

But he was correct about our history and founding national character: *openness to the new was a defining American trait.* From the start, four centuries ago, we were eager to try the untried and explore the uncharted, even or especially when it looked risky or terrifying. Americans' innovative, novelty-seeking, risk-taking attitudes were key to most of the country's exceptional successes. The United States was a self-consciously new species of nation, the first one invented from scratch and based on new conceptions of freedom and fairness and self-government and national identity. Our story at its best was a process of collectively, successfully imagining, embracing, and exemplifying the new—then gloating whenever the rest of the world followed our lead.

Of course, that process of perpetual reinvention and refreshment always involved tension between people pushing for the new and people resisting it, sometimes with existential ferocity: irreconcilable differences over status quos resulted first in the American Revolution and then in the Civil War and then the politics of the Depression. In our history so far, at the critical junctures, the forces of the new have eventually triumphed over the anciens régimes.

Almost a half-century ago, the country began a strange hiatus from its founding mission of inventing and reinventing itself in pursuit of the new and improved. Since then Americans have gotten variously confused and contentious and paralyzed concerning the old days, about which parts of the American past can or can't and should or shouldn't be restored. So the essential new national project I'm proposing here is paradoxical: a majority of us have got to rediscover and revive the old defining American predisposition to reject old certainties and familiar ways, plunge forward, experiment, imagine, and then try the untried.

It's important to revisit and dissect and understand what happened when this rigging began and the swamp was filled, and not just to know who to blame for our present predicament. Rather, as we attempt to fix the terrible mess that an unbalanced, unhinged, decadent capitalism has an economy of cybernated abundance that does not need their labor." In general the utopians at that giddy moment didn't very carefully address how capitalism in the United States and other countries would have to change to avoid Wiener's economic future of unmitigated cruelty.

As the 1970s began, the cultural and political Sixties were still going full tilt, accelerating. Single-sex colleges were all rushing to go co-ed—Princeton, Yale, Bennington, and Kenyon in 1969, Johns Hopkins, Colgate, the University of Virginia, and Williams in 1970. A year earlier a half-million young people had assembled for Woodstock, a new species of American event, and another, record-breaking half-million had assembled in Washington, D.C., to protest the Vietnam War. The New Left spun off a terrorist faction that was setting off an average of ten bombs a week in government buildings and banks around America. A constitutional amendment to lower the voting age from twenty-one to eighteen was about to be passed by Congress (unanimously in the Senate, 401–19 in the House), then ratified by the states in a hundred days, faster than any amendment before or since. Congress promptly passed another constitutional amendment, one to guarantee equal rights for women, by margins almost as large.

Given how much had changed during just the last few years, if that tidal wave of new continued through the 1970s—and why wouldn't it?—what additional shocking changes might lie just ahead?

In fact, in the early 1970s, we had reached Peak New.

PART TWO

Turning Point

4

_{⊹⊹⊹⊹⊹⊹⊹⊹⊹⊹⊹⊹}

The 1970s:
An Equal and Opposite Reaction

"Everything happened during the sixties," the dystopian fiction writer J. G. Ballard said after they ended. He'd turned thirty in 1961, the optimal age to be a trustworthy real-time chronicler of that decade.* "Thanks to TV, you got strange overlaps between the assassinations and Vietnam and the space race and the youth pop explosion and psychedelia and the drug culture. It was like a huge amusement park going out of control."

I was only fifteen at the end of the 1960s, but it really was like that, even though not the *entire* park was haywire, and some astoundingly great new attractions (civil rights, expanded social welfare, feminism, and environmentalism) were being built at the same time. *Future Shock,* published in the summer of 1970, became one of the bestselling books of the decade. "This is a book about what happens to people when they are overwhelmed by change," wrote the authors, whose lecture in Omaha I excitedly attended at fifteen, "the shattering stress and disorientation that we induce in individuals by submitting them to too much change in too

---

*Norman Mailer was a bit older, thirty-six as the decade began, but Tom Wolfe turned thirty in 1960, Joan Didion in 1964, and Hunter Thompson in 1967.

short a time," the "roaring current of change . . . so powerful today that it overturns institutions [and] shifts our values."

At that same moment, as the besotted forty-two-year-old Professor Reich at Yale published *The Greening of America,* the more typical reaction to the tumult was that of Harvard's fifty-one-year-old professor Daniel Bell, definitely not feeling groovy. "No one in our post-modern culture is on the side of order or tradition," he wrote in a famous essay called "The Cultural Contradictions of Capitalism." He despaired that the "traditional bourgeois organization of life—its rationalism and sobriety—no longer has any defenders in the culture."

As with all zeitgeists, not everybody and probably not even most people were entirely on board with the spirit of the time. Frightened and angry reactions to the culturally and politically new had germinated instantly. For many people during the 1960s, the perpetual novelty that had been at the heart of modern American capitalism and modern American culture changed from amazing and grand to disconcerting and traumatic. What Marx and Engels had written 120 years earlier about capitalism's collateral impacts was coming true, too true—*all fixed relations swept away, all new-formed ones antiquated before they can ossify, all that is holy profaned, all that is solid melts into air.* In culture, Bell wrote in that 1970 essay, there was now an overriding

> impulse towards the new and the original, a self-conscious search
> for future forms and sensations. . . . Society now . . . has provided
> a market which eagerly gobbles up the new, because it believes
> it to be superior in value to all older forms. Thus, our culture has
> an unprecedented mission: it is an official, ceaseless searching for
> a new sensibility. . . . A society given over entirely to innovation,
> in the joyful acceptance of change, has in fact institutionalized an
> *avant-garde* and charged it—perhaps to its own eventual dismay—
> with constantly turning up something new. . . . There exists only a
> desire for the new.

As people get older, they do tend to lose interest in the new. And what I call Peak New has a statistical demographic underpinning: Americans' median age had been in the teens and twenties for our whole history, and it was dropping again in the 1950s and '60s—but then after 1970 it began increasing, quickly, the average American getting two or three years older each decade. By 1990 it reached thirty-three, higher than it had ever been, and it has continued going up toward middle age.

During the 1970s, just coming off the '60s and their relentless avant-gardism, people really did feel exhausted, ready to relax and be reassured. Even lots of people who were delighted by the 1960s, by the new laws intended to increase equality and fairness and by the loosey-goosier new laissez-faire cultural sensibilities and norms, were in a kind of bewildered morning-after slough. In response, more and more Americans began looking back fondly to times before the late 1960s, times that seemed by comparison so reassuringly familiar and calm and coherent. In other words, that curious old American nostalgia tic expressed itself as it hadn't for decades—in fact, it took over with an intensity and longevity it never had before. The multiple shocks of the new triggered a wide-ranging reversion to the old. It turned out Isaac Newton's third law of motion operates in the social universe as well as physics: the 1960s actions had been sudden and powerful, and the reactions starting in the 1970s were equal and opposite, with follow-on effects that lasted much, much longer.

Some of the origins of this 1970s plunge into nostalgia, in fact, had showed themselves a bit earlier. Paradoxically, as America was approaching Peak New during the 1950s and '60s, some members of the cultural avant-garde led the way in making the past seem stylish, embracing certain bits and pieces of the old days in order to be unorthodox, *counter*cultural, cooler. It was selective stylistic nostalgia as a way of going against the grain, rejecting earnest upbeat spic-and-span corporate suburban midcentury America. Back in the 1950s, when *vintage* applied only to wine and automobiles, the Beats and beatniks had bought and proudly worn used clothes from the 1920s and '30s. Jack Kerouac's *On the Road*, the classic cutting-edge Beat novel, is actually an exercise in nostalgia, as the critic Louis Menand says, published and set in 1957 but actually "a book about the nineteen-forties," the "dying . . . world of hoboes and migrant workers and cowboys and crazy joyriders." His cool 1950s characters, Kerouac wrote, all shared "a sentimental streak about the old days in America, . . . when the country was wild and brawling and free, with abundance and any kind of freedom for everyone," and the character Old Bull Lee's "chief hate was Washington bureaucracy; second to that, liberals; then cops." The simultaneous folk-music revival, from which Bob Dylan emerged, also consisted of cool kids scratching the same nostalgic American itch ahead of everyone else. College students and hepcats in the early 1960s also rediscovered and worshiped 1940s movies like *Casablanca* and *The Maltese Falcon* at smoky revival movie theaters.

In 1964 Kerouac's road-trip buddy Neal Cassady joined young Ken Kesey and his band of protohippies, driving them across America from the Santa Cruz Mountains to New York City to visit, yes, the World's Fair. They were pioneering inventors of the counterculture—which presently became a mass phenomenon and inherited some of the Beats' sentimental streaks concerning the American old days. Even as youth circa 1970 thought of themselves as shock troops of a new age, part of their shocking newness was nostalgic cosplay. Dressed in reproduction nineteenth-century artifacts—blue jeans, fringed leather jackets, boots, bandanas, hats, men mustachioed and bearded—they fancied themselves hoboes and cowboys and joyriders and agrarian anarchists as they got high and listened to "Maggie's Farm" (Bob Dylan), "Up on Cripple Creek" (the Band), and "Uncle John's Band" (the Grateful Dead). Overnight they made the uncool old Victorian houses in San Francisco cool. The vision of the future sold starting in 1968 by the *Whole Earth Catalog,* the counterculture's obligatory omnibus almanac, was agrarian and handmade as well as—*so* ahead of the curve—computerized and video-recorded.

In 1969, at the Woodstock Festival, the music of the final performer, Jimi Hendrix, was absolute late '60s, disconcertingly and deliciously freaky and vain. Playing right before him, however, had been a group almost nobody knew. Sha Na Na, led by a Columbia University graduate student, sang cover versions of a dozen rock and doo-wop songs from 1956 to 1963, wearing 1950s-style costumes and doing 1950s-style choreography. To the crowd and to the *Woodstock* movie audiences in 1970, this was spectacularly surprising and amusing. It was intense *instant* nostalgia, a measure of just how much and how quickly everything had changed. Songs only six or twelve years old, the music of their childhoods and earlier adolescence—"Jailhouse Rock," "The Book of Love," "At the Hop," "Teen Angel," "Duke of Earl"—already seemed *so ridiculously dated.* Even at the event that remains a defining peak moment of a revolutionary new age that had only just gotten started—the phrase *Woodstock Generation* actually preceded *baby boomers*—Americans began turning backward for the reassuring, unchallenging gaze back at a past that wouldn't change or surprise or shock.

Nostalgia was the charming sanctuary to which people retreated to feel better during their post-1960s hangover—and then never really left. They were encouraged by a culture industry that immediately created a wide-ranging nostalgia division of a kind that hadn't existed before.

The Last Picture Show, set in 1951, came out in 1971, made tons of money, and won Oscars. The musical *Grease,* set in 1959, appeared in 1971, became the most popular movie of 1978 (featuring Sha Na Na, who by then had their own popular TV variety show), and ran on Broadway for the whole decade. *The Way We Were,* the fifth most popular movie of 1973, was set mainly in the 1950s. George Lucas's *American Graffiti,* set in 1962, was the third most popular movie of 1973 and softened the ground for the premiere a few months later of its TV doppelgänger *Happy Days,* which in 1976 spun off *Laverne & Shirley,* set in the late 1950s and early '60s. *Animal House,* also set in 1962, came out in the late 1970s and was one of the most successful movies of the decade.

"I saw rock and roll future and its name is Bruce Springsteen," an influential young rock critic wrote in a review of a live performance in 1974, then helped make it so by becoming his producer for two decades. Hearing the seventy-year-old Springsteen singing his songs today, rhapsodizing about characters and tales of his youth, the nostalgia seems earned and real. But back in the early 1970s, as a twenty-four-year-old, he came across as a superior nostalgia act, an earnest higher-IQ Fonzie. He "seems somewhat anachronistic to many—black leather jacket, street-poet, kids-on-the-run, guitar as switchblade," another influential young rock critic wrote in his positive review of *Born to Run* in 1975. "Springsteen is not an innovator—his outlook is rooted in the Fifties; his music comes out of early rock 'n' roll, his lyrics from 1950s teenage rebellion movies and beat poetry."

It wasn't just the American 1950s on which American pop culture suddenly, lovingly gorged in the 1970s. *Every era* became a nostalgic fetish object. During the 1970s, fans of the Grateful Dead began bathing in nostalgia for the late 1960s, "obsessively stockpiling audio documentation of the live Dead," as the cultural historian Simon Reynolds explains, indulging their "deepest impulse: to freeze-frame History and artificially keep alive an entire era." And that has continued into the twenty-first century—"the gentle frenzy of Deadheads is a ghost dance: an endangered, out-of-time people willing a lost world back into existence."

"Everything Old Is New Again" became a pop hit in 1974 for a reason. *The Godfather* (1972) fetishized the look and feel of the 1940s, *The Great Gatsby* (1974) of the 1920s—and at the heart of both were notions central to the emerging American economic zeitgeist: "It's not personal, it's strictly business," as Michael Corleone said, and greed and ostentatious wealth and gangsterism were all hereby cool. Most of the earnest bits in Woody Allen's work consist of nostalgia, starting in 1972 with *Play It Again Sam. Most* of the most popular movies released in 1973 trafficked in twentieth-century nostalgia, including the gorgeous Depression of *The Sting* and *Paper Moon. The Waltons,* a sentimental TV drama set during the Depression and World War II in a small Virginia town, premiered in 1972 and ran until 1981. Even the one enduring *new* Hollywood genre that arose in the mid-1970s and early '80s, what Lucas and Steven Spielberg created with *Star Wars* and *Raiders of the Lost Ark,* was actually just a big-budget revival of an old genre, forgettable action-adventure B movies and serials from the 1930s and '40s and '50s.

In the 1970s I was too young to perceive this sudden total national immersion in nostalgia as unprecedented and meaningful, so I've wondered since if it only looks like that in retrospect. I was therefore delighted, as I was almost finished with this book, to discover a somewhat shocked contemporaneous account of the phenomenon. It's a remarkable Rosetta Stone.

Robert Brustein, the dean of the Yale School of Drama at the time, published a magazine essay in 1975 called "Retread Culture." Back then, by today's standards, revivals and remakes and multiple sequels were still extremely rare. The first modern superhero movie (*Superman,* 1978) hadn't yet been made. But Brustein was struck by the strangeness of "the current nostalgia boom," the "revivals of old stage hits," "retrospectives of films from the thirties and forties by auteur directors, authentic looking reconstructions of period styles in new films," "revived musical forms," and so on. "Much of contemporary American entertainment," he wrote, "is not so much being created as re-created," each "recycled commodity" presented in the place of something actually new.

And he connected this change in popular culture to changes in political and social sentiment, as some kind of reaction to "a deep American discontent with the present time." This was still five years before Reagan was elected president.

> The culture is partially reflecting America's current conservative mood. A nation which always looked forward is now in the process of looking backward, with considerable longing for the real or imagined comforts of the past. Where audiences once were eager for what was novel and innovative, they now seem more comfortable with the familiar, as if they wished to escape from contemporary difficulties into the more reassuring territory of the habitual and the known.

He saw too that what made the nostalgia different than earlier blips of cultural revivalism was "its multiplicity and universality," turning out reproduction antiques in every part of the culture.

> Why, it is even becoming difficult to identify a distinctive look for our age which is not a compound of past fashions. The cut of our trousers, the shape of our dresses, the style of our furs, coiffures, cosmetics and jewelry, our very advertising techniques and printing models, are all derived from earlier periods—a mishmash of the frontier West, Art Deco, and the flapper era.

Brustein mentioned E. L. Doctorow's fine novel *Ragtime,* a big bestseller at the time that was also esteemed by the elite, about to win the very first National Book Critics Circle Award for fiction. Historical fiction hadn't been considered *literary* fiction for quite a while, but suddenly it was respectable again.

Seeming to be strikingly modern wasn't exactly the same as looking like something from the future, but the two had frequently overlapped during the twentieth century, especially in design and art—in the 1930s, for instance, the concrete slabs of Frank Lloyd Wright's Fallingwater and Raymond Loewy's streamlined locomotives were both. That overlap of the new and the futuristic maxed out in 1964 and 1965, the World's Fair years, the years the newly coined phrases *Jet Age* and *Space Age* achieved their peak usage. The hot women's fashion line of 1964 consisted of short Lycra-and-plastic dresses printed with giant bright stripes and dots. In

fashion, Simon Reynolds suggests that 1965 was "the absolute pinnacle
of Newness and Nowness." In the later 1960s, "almost overnight, everything stopped looking futuristic" in fashion and instead became riffs on
the exotically foreign or—because in the '60s the past was an especially
foreign country—the bygone "Victoriana, Edwardiana, twenties and thirties influences." All at once, the past started to seem charming to many
more people, while purely excited, hopeful visions of the future came to
seem naïve or absurd.*

Earlier I mentioned midcentury urban renewal as an example of
America's love for the new turning single-minded and reckless. It was
like an autoimmune disease, when misguided antibodies destroy healthy
human tissue. But even as that demolition of old buildings and neighborhoods was going full speed, local activists (in New York City most of all)
and a few enlightened owners (in Omaha, for instance) started to beat it
back—another example of how American citizens have placed essential
checks and balances on excessive and misguided power. *The Death and
Life of Great American Cities,* by the Manhattan journalist-turned-activist
Jane Jacobs, became the manifesto of a successful and powerful new
movement in 1961; by the end of the decade, historic preservation was
fully institutionalized, and in the 1970s saving and renovating nice old
buildings and neighborhoods was becoming the default.†

At the same moment, architecture and urban planning rediscovered
the amusements and lessons of history. Architects were designing *new*
buildings with columns and pitched roofs and pediments and colorful
finishes—a so-called postmodern reaction by elite architects, who used
the old-fashioned design moves and materials that the modernist elite
had declared taboo for half a century. What began in the late 1960s and
'70s as fond, bemused takes on old architectural styles morphed during

*Which is why starting in the 1970s, for instance, the humorist and illustrator Bruce
McCall could have a career painting panoramas of fantastical flying machines and infrastructure for the *National Lampoon* and then *The New Yorker,* grand futures as if depicted
by overoptimists of the past, what he called "retro-futurism."
†Between 1964 and 1969, university architecture schools began teaching preservation;
the first old American factory was turned into a warren of upscale shops (in Ghirardelli
Square in San Francisco); the Manhattan neighborhood where artists had started moving into old industrial lofts was named SoHo, and New York City created a commission
that could prevent developers from demolishing historic buildings and neighborhoods;
Congress passed the National Historic Preservation Act; and Seattle created the Pioneer
Square Historic District.

the '80s into no-kidding reproductions of buildings from the good old days. Serious architects and planners calling themselves New Urbanists convinced developers to build entirely new towns (first and most notably Seaside, Florida), urban neighborhoods (such as Carlyle in Alexandria, Virginia), and suburban extensions (The Crossings in Mountain View, California) that looked and felt like they had been built fifty or one hundred years earlier, with narrow streets and back alleys and front porches. A convincingly faux-old baseball park, Camden Yards in Baltimore, established a new default design for American stadiums.

That two-step rediscovery of the past—at first amused and a bit ironic, but soon wholeheartedly sincere, making the old and uncool cool and then *normal*—was a sensibility shift made by tens of millions of lifestylizing Americans not yet known as the creative class. During the 1970s, *retro* became a trendy word.

The Official Preppy Handbook became a crypto-nostalgic bestseller in 1980 by good-naturedly satirizing a certain archaic strain of rich white American privilege as if the 1960s cultural upheavals hadn't happened. Everyone started using the new term *comfort food,* only a bit ironically, to destigmatize old-fashioned American dishes that were familiar, unchallenging, unvirtuous—biscuits, cupcakes, meatloaf, grits, mashed potatoes, macaroni and cheese. The meaning was soon extended to celebrate any and all of our newly unshackled and unapologetic tastes for the old and familiar. J. G. Ballard wrote that right after World War II, which ended when he was fifteen, "people simply became uninterested in the past"—*until* the 1970s, he noticed in the 1990s, when suddenly "nobody was interested in the future. Now they are only interested in the past in a sort of theme-park-like way. They ransack the past for the latest design statement."

But as it turned out, not just for design statements and lifestyle inspirations. Thirty years ago my friend Paul Rudnick and I wrote a cover story for *Spy* about how the recent spate of "Hollywood nostalgia productions [had] portrayed the fifties and early sixties as something to be pined for, something cute and pastel colored and fun rather than racist and oppressive." And how in the 1980s, when we were writing, the new omnipresent nostalgia meant that "you can become Dan Quayle," the forty-two-year-old conservative Republican vice president, "or you can become part of the irony epidemic. Or if you're of a mind to organize an absolutely nutty

George Hamilton memorial limbo competition at the country club, *both*."
In other words, post-1960s irony turned out to be "a way for all kinds of
taboo styles to sneak past the taste authorities—*don't mind us, we're just
kidding*—and then, once inside, turn serious." America in the 1970s and
'80s gave itself permission not only to celebrate the old days but also to re-
produce and *restore* them. Picking and choosing and exploiting elements
of the past extended to politics and the political economy.

To understand how that worked, how the opening of the nostalgia floodgates throughout culture helped the political tide to turn as well, it's useful to look back barely a generation—when it spectacularly *failed* to work
in the *early* 1960s. The national political right had tried demonizing liberal modernity before enough Americans were fatigued or appalled by
accelerating newness for politicians to exploit that reaction successfully.

Barry Goldwater—a conservative Republican when that wasn't redundant, a not-very-religious right-winger when that wasn't an oxymoron,
a libertarian before they were called that—halfheartedly tried to use the
incipient cultural backlash when he ran for president in 1964. He'd gotten into politics fighting the New Deal when it was still new, and ever
since had advocated for the U.S. economy taking a sharp right turn or full
U-turn back to the days before the 1930s. Milton Friedman, an avatar of
that ultra-conservative economic strain the same age as Goldwater, was one
of his advisers when he was the Republican nominee, the most right-wing
nominee ever. He proposed cutting personal and corporate income taxes by
25 percent for starters, scrapping new and imminent socialist programs like
Medicare and food stamps, keeping Social Security from getting any more
generous, and ending "this cancerous growth of the federal government."

The political economy (including maximum anti-Communism) was
his overriding focus. But none of that appeared in the half-hour campaign
ad that a team of Goldwater operatives produced and bought time to run
on 150 NBC stations just before the 1964 election. The film is an extraor-
dinary artifact, remarkably ahead of the curve for its hysterical depiction
of the scary new—teenagers, black people, protests, unbelievers, cos-
mopolitanism run amok. It was a propaganda ur-text for today's ongoing
American culture war, which at the time almost nobody considered a war.
It tied together and sensationally stoked all of the embryonic backlashes.

The film starts without narration for ninety seconds, just an exciting quick-cut montage of young people doing the Twist, a crowd of black people singing on a city street, cops arresting people, a pair of apparently gay men, topless go-go dancers, all intercut with shots of a recklessly speeding car and with a soundtrack of frenzied rock guitar riffs. As the narrator begins his voice-over, cut to the Statue of Liberty, a small town and its church, white children obediently pledging allegiance to the flag—then cut back to another frenzied montage of black people protesting and being arrested and some white people having too much fun, in particular dancing women shot from behind or without tops. That's the structure of the entire thirty-minute film, three parts decadence interposed with one part good-old-fashioned America, back and forth. "Now there are *two* Americas," the narrator begins,

> the other America—the other America is no longer a dream, but a *nightmare.* . . . Our streets are not safe, immorality begins to flourish—we don't want this. . . . The new America—ask not what you can give but what you can *take.* . . . Illegitimate births swell the relief rolls. . . . Teenagers read the headlines, see the TV news, anything goes now. . . . They see the cancer of pornography festering.

Cut to an extremely long sequence of porn film posters, strip club marquees, and paperback covers including *Call Me Nympho, Jazz Me Baby,* and *Male for Sale.* All of which were, in fact, public rarities.

> But the new America says, "This is free speech." In the new America the ancient moral law is mocked. "Nation under God—who's He?" . . . No longer is a uniform a symbol of authority. The rules of the game have been changed now. . . . Up through the courts of law, justice becomes a sick joke, new loopholes allegedly protecting freedom now turn more and more criminals free on the nation's streets. . . . By new laws it's not the *lawbreaker* who is handcuffed, it is the *police.* . . . Vigilante committees, good citizens, grope for a solution.

Cut to shots of the U.S.-Mexican border—from more than half a century ago.

Over the borders—*dope*. Narcotics traffic setting a new depraved record. And the victims so often are the defenseless—the kids. . . . How did this happen? Is there a reason we seemed to have changed so much in so short a time?

A *really* short time—according to this film, the moral decay got bad only during the previous eleven months, since the assassination of the "young, inspiring" President Kennedy. After NBC asked for deletions of "60 of the most risqué seconds," Goldwater at the last moment decided not to air the film, even though his campaign sent two hundred prints to conservative groups to show all over the country.

He lost by a landslide to President Lyndon Johnson, of course, whose share of the vote remains the largest ever. At the time one takeaway was that right-wing economic ideas were a total political nonstarter, anachronisms that would remain so. But in fact the Goldwater campaign was just the first rollout of a new American political template, an unsuccessful beta test. It tried to exploit popular unease with the culturally new as a way to get a green light for the rollback that Goldwater and the serious right *really* cared about—a restoration of old-style economic and tax and regulatory policies tilted toward business and the well-to-do.

That lashing of cultural fear to political economics was just ahead of its time. Because 1964 was before the proliferation of hippies and marijuana and psychedelics, before a large feminist movement emerged and workplaces started filling with unprecedented numbers of women. It was before U.S. combat forces went to Vietnam, before the antiwar movement blossomed. It was before violent crime really shot up—murders in the United States increased by half during the five years from 1964 to 1969, and in New York City by that much in just two years, from 1966 to 1968.

Goldwater's landslide defeat was before the epic black uprisings that came later in the 1960s (Watts, Newark, Detroit) along with the black power movement. But it was just after a couple of years of spectacular civil rights demonstrations and confrontations and *immediately* after the Civil Rights Act became law—which is why the Goldwater film had so many shots of unruly black people and why five of the six states Goldwater won were in the Deep South.

It was also before a critical mass of white people outside the South started feeling the way most white Southerners felt—besieged by blacks, their whiteness no longer quite such a guaranteed all-access VIP pass. It was before wallowing in nostalgia for a lost Golden Age ruined by meddling liberal outsiders from Washington and New York, previously a white Southern habit, became such a common white *American* habit. It was before respectable opinion, having spent a century trying to make ethnic tribalism seem anachronistic and wrong, began accepting and embracing a lot of it. "One of the central themes in the culture of the 1970s was the rehabilitation of ethnic memory and history as a vital part of personal identity," the leftist professor Marshall Berman wrote in his wonderful 1982 book *All That Is Solid Melts into Air: The Experience of Modernity.* "This has been a striking development in the history of modernity. Modernists today no longer insist, as the modernists of yesterday so often did, that we must cease to be Jewish, or black, or Italian, or anything, in order to be modern."

Goldwater was trounced before fantasies about the old days became a craze and then a national cultural default. As he prepared to announce his presidential candidacy, the Arizona department store heir appeared on the cover of *Life* magazine—circulation 8 million, 1960s America's single most respectably glamorous mass media pedestal—wearing a cowboy hat, work shirt, and blue jeans, cuddling his horse. But like his OMG-decadence-black-people-chaos film, that too was ahead of its time in 1963—more than a decade before the post-1960s nostalgic counterreaction made a majority of Americans ready to fall hard for a prospective Old West president in a Marlboro Man getup.

By 1971, however, nostalgia was seriously cross-fertilizing with grassroots political attitudes. That's when the comedy *All in the Family* went on the air and became for six years the most popular American television show. The premise was Archie Bunker's perpetual politicized anger at post-1960s America, but the show's theme song, sung by the Bunker character and his wife, was a piece of cutting-edge nostalgia combining resentment *and* fondness about politics *and* culture.

Didn't need no welfare state . . .
Girls were girls and men were men

Mister, we could use a man like Herbert Hoover again . . .
I don't know just what went wrong
Those were the days

Richard Nixon won the presidency twice, in 1968 and 1972, but both times mainly due to Archie Bunkerism, to reaction against the 1960s' cultural tumult and new civil rights policies, *not* out of any popular cry for freer markets. In 1968, Nixon and his Democratic opponent, Hubert Humphrey, received essentially identical fractions of the vote, but sociologically it wasn't close: the combined vote of Nixon and George Wallace, the white-supremacist third-party candidate, was 57 percent, an anti-hippie-anti-Negro-anti-crime landslide. In 1972 Nixon won in an actual landslide over his Democratic opponent, Senator George McGovern— 61 percent of the vote, forty-nine states, still the third-biggest margin in U.S. presidential election history—because hippies were still proliferating and antiwar protests and bombings by New Left fugitives were still happening.*

The nightmare of the new that had been depicted in 1964 in that Goldwater film had been more than realized in just eight years—LSD! free love! Woodstock! blasphemy! women's lib! gay rights! anti-Americanism! riots! bombings!—and was now at the center of the conservative political pitch. Some of those visceral negative reflexes in the late 1960s— confusion, disgust, anger—had started to congeal, become fixed. Many of the people who'd had strong spontaneous reactions in 1967 had by 1972 turned into full-on cultural reactionaries, actively encouraged by the organized political right.

The sloganeering had improved. "A spirit of national masochism prevails," Nixon's vice president famously said, "encouraged by an effete corps of impudent snobs who characterize themselves as intellectuals." In the spring of 1972, during the primaries, a liberal Democratic senator was anonymously quoted in an article warning that "the people don't know McGovern is for amnesty, abortion, and legalization of pot."

---

*And the anti-civil-rights backlash was still erupting: George Wallace ran in 1972 in the *Democratic* primaries and won six states, including Michigan and Maryland, and got almost as many votes in all as McGovern.

The Nixonians condensed that into an effective alliterative caricature of McGovernism—Acid, Amnesty, and Abortion.*

Paradoxically, the other big reason President Nixon got reelected by such an enormous margin in 1972 was because on policy he did not swim against the lingering, dominant leftward ideological tide. Unlike Goldwater, he wasn't committed to a superaggressive global anti-Communist crusade but instead oversaw the slow-motion U.S. surrender in Vietnam ("peace with honor") and the remarkable U.S. diplomatic opening to Communist China and détente with the Soviet Union. Unlike the Goldwater right (as I'll discuss in the next chapter), he definitely did not try to roll back Johnson's Great Society social welfare programs, let alone FDR's New Deal. His administration actually built upon them. He wasn't a liberal, just a canny, stone-cold cynic going with the liberal flow.

Economic equality, as a result of all those countervailing forces I talked about, was at its peak in the mid-1970s. It was the same in the United States then as it is in Scandinavian countries today, the share of the nation's wealth owned by nonwealthy Americans larger than it had been since measurements began. The system was working pretty well, and the national consensus about fairness endured. People took for granted all the progress we'd achieved. It really seemed irreversible.

*In fact, McGovern supported marijuana decriminalization, not legalization; blanket amnesty for draft resisters but not military deserters; and each state continuing to decide its own abortion laws. And the Democratic senator who so effectively slagged him behind his back, Thomas Eagleton, became his vice-presidential nominee.

ingly self-concerned and even cynical, is not impressed by . . . the smooth
theatrical conservative nostalgia of Ronald Reagan." Yet over the next
month Reagan ran an extremely close second to President Ford in the
Iowa and New Hampshire primaries and very nearly won the nomination.
As that presidential election got going, another leading political journalist
noted that "layered over everything" in the political landscape "are apathy,
nostalgia and cynicism."

Reston's idol Walter Lippmann, the great American political com-
mentator and author who'd recently died, had derided politicized nostalgia sixty years earlier, at the beginning of his career and the modern
age. "Men generally find in the past what they miss in the present," he
wrote.

> For most of us insist that somewhere in the past there was a golden
> age. But people who are forever dreaming of a mythical past are
> merely saying that they are afraid of the future. The past which
> men create for themselves is a place where thought is unnecessary
> and happiness is inevitable. The American temperament leans
> generally to a kind of mystical anarchism.

In 1976 the Republicans were not yet the party of unhinged mystical
anarchism they became over the next four decades. Rather, after the un-
happiness, unfriendliness, cynicism, paranoia, and finally the high crimes
of Richard Nixon, Americans were eager to install Mr. Rogers in the
White House—that is, sincere, low-key, straightforward Jimmy Carter, a
devoutly Protestant goody-goody complete with toothy smile and cardi-
gan sweater whom Reston hadn't even mentioned as a contender in his
New Year's election preview.

The choice was between two basically boring, moderate nice guys
whom nobody'd heard of a couple of years earlier—a governor running
against Washington, Carter, and a lifelong Washington congressional
hack who stepped in to replace Nixon's criminal vice president and then
pardoned Nixon for his crimes, Gerald Ford. Not only did Carter appear to be Nixon's opposite, he also seemed to fit the zeitgeist's nostalgia
requirement: a farmer from a small town called Plains, a Sunday school
teacher, and on race a latter-day Atticus Finch.

Electing Jimmy Carter in the fall of 1976 was a natural follow-up to the U.S. bicentennial summer. The bicentennial commemorations were a surprisingly big-deal reboot of national solidarity—a Fourth of July nostalgiapalooza that came along at a ripe moment. In addition to the two hundredth national birthday party, they served as a de facto celebration of the end of the Sixties hangover that had included the finales of Vietnam (1975) and Watergate (1974). I'd just graduated college and arrived in New York City, where people—jaded, sophisticated *New Yorkers*—were fully, enthusiastically engaged in this Americana spectacle. The Grand Parade of Sailing Ships, sixteen old square-riggers each a hundred yards long, gliding into the harbor as if from out of the nineteenth century and past the Statue of Liberty! Plus dozens of military ships disgorging thousands of excited sailors all over the city, *On the Town* come to life!

But after hopeful visions of old-fashioned American virtue helped elect him, Jimmy Carter couldn't manage to play the nostalgia card worth a damn, and *President* Carter never came across as a leading man. Americans don't require presidents (or leading men) to be cheerful or manly all the time, but in the modern era they really can't abide mopes and wimps and scolds.

The previous paradigm shift in the U.S. political economy, embodied and enacted by the New Deal in the 1930s, had been triggered by economic catastrophe—a quarter of all workers suddenly unemployed, the pay of the ones still working significantly cut, savings wiped out by the failures of almost half the banks, stock prices down 89 percent in three years. Nothing remotely as horrible as the Great Depression happened in the 1970s to persuade Americans to make a sharp right turn or reverse course from the country the New Deal had built. Our successful free-market system, as rebuilt in the 1930s and tweaked since, had not teetered or collapsed. In fact, despite a recession, the 1970s were a great decade for business: from 1970 to 1979, corporate profits overall nearly doubled, getting higher than they'd been since 1951. Inequality was as moderate as it had been in the twentieth century. But two very unpleasant and unfamiliar new economic conditions—high inflation year after year and much higher-priced oil and gasoline—made citizens more willing to accept big changes in the economy.

For the three decades since the Truman administration, inflation had been practically imperceptible, mostly running between 1 and 3 percent, as it is in the twenty-first century and has been for three decades. But from 1973 to 1975, the annual rate of inflation rose from less than 4 percent to more than 12 percent, and in 1980 it nearly reached 15 percent. The prices of everything were increasing by half or more every few years. Inflation made for a sense of out-of-control flux that almost nobody enjoyed, as if the 1960s' dismaying rate of change were continuing but without any of the good or fun parts. In a decade, prices more than doubled, meaning that the value of cash savings shrank by more than half. Interest rates on loans naturally doubled as well. Many Americans were disconcerted, angry, and a little panicky. If your middle-class salary doubled between 1973 and 1980, for instance, your purchasing power didn't actually increase *at all,* and yet because of inflation, your marginal federal tax rate could have gone from 24 to 30 percent. Which might well incline you in the next election to vote for the candidates of a Republican Party that was starting to make lower taxes its central promise.

When inflation had begun creeping higher at the end of the 1960s, the economy was still growing fast. But in the mid-1970s there was a double whammy—crazily inflating prices were accompanied by a long economic recession, a combination so unusual the new word *stagflation* was coined. In fact, it was a triple whammy: during the 1970s in America (as in the whole developed world), a *post*–post–World War II slowdown in growth and productivity was becoming apparent. During a single recessionary year, 100,000 U.S. steelworkers were laid off. But even during a more economically ordinary year, 1979, the auto industry laid off a third of its workforce.

The mid-'70s recession had been triggered by a sudden quadrupling of oil prices by OPEC, the dozen-nation cartel that produced most of the world's petroleum. Yet for Americans, the oil crisis wasn't just about the oil crisis and the higher gasoline and home heating prices—it was routinely called the *Arab* oil crisis. OPEC consisted of *third world* countries, and we were also months away from officially losing our disastrous decade-long war to a third world country, North Vietnam. On multiple fronts, the end of America's twentieth-century invincibility suddenly seemed nigh.

While there was nothing in the 1970s economically comparable to the Depression to trigger an equivalent political about-face, there were several simultaneous and mutually reinforcing narratives about our failing national moxie. The federal government seemed manifestly incompetent *and* weak, both at home *and* abroad, *and*—don't forget Watergate, don't forget the new revelations of FBI and CIA misdeeds—*evil* to boot. *It didn't used to be this way. Why can't things be like they used to be?*

The pivotal year for the energized economic right was 1978. Its dreams were starting to come true. Americans were now more skeptical of government than of big business. At the beginning of the year a CBS News/ *New York Times* survey found that 58 percent of Americans agreed that "the Government has gone too far in regulating business and interfering with the free enterprise system," up from 42 percent during the 1960s.

A critical mass of the people elected to run the government had also been persuaded to give big business what it wanted. Democrats held the presidency and a two-to-one House majority and a historic sixty-two-seat Senate majority. Yet in early 1978, a bill to create a new consumer protection agency was defeated in the House because 101 Democrats voted against it, including a majority of the Democratic freshmen, thanks in large part to lobbying by CEOs from the Business Roundtable.

And 1978 was also a tipping-point year in the economic right's crusade to persuade people that because government now sucked, all taxes paid to all governments by everyone, no matter how wealthy, were way too high and also sucked. The overwhelmingly Democratic Congress overwhelmingly passed and the Democratic president signed into law a huge reduction in taxes on income from selling stocks, capital gains—a definitive turn toward making extra-sure the rich got richer faster. Just five years earlier, when he was governor of California, Ronald Reagan had pushed a ballot initiative to cut and permanently limit various state and local taxes; it was decisively defeated. In 1978 Proposition 13, a California state constitutional amendment to cut property taxes by more than half and permanently limit increases, was decisively approved.

Carter was elected as the sweet, honest anti-Nixon. Ironically, the rapid zeitgeist shift of the 1970s meant that after a Republican who'd governed as a liberal, certainly by the standards ever since, his immediate successor governed as "the most conservative Democratic President since Grover Cleveland," according to the liberal historian Arthur Schlesinger, Jr. But conservatives weren't buying it, any more than liberals had bought Nixon's liberalism. By the summer of 1979, even though he'd presided over no disasters (yet), only about 30 percent of people told pollsters they approved of the job the president was doing, fewer than for any postwar president so far except Nixon in his final Watergate year.

So how did Carter respond? By canceling a big televised Fourth of July Oval Office address at the last minute and spending the next ten days writing a new one. His call to action was austerity, reducing our use of imported oil—not for environmental reasons but because oil had gotten so expensive. The speech, however, was like a scene from a remake of *Mr. Smith Goes to Washington* written by and starring Wallace Shawn. Carter spent the first two-thirds on a half-hour jeremiad about America's "crisis of confidence," wondering "why have we not been able to get together as a nation," bewailing "the growing doubt about the meaning of our own lives" and "a system of government that seems incapable of action"—but it's worse than that, he said, because "all the legislation in the world can't fix what's wrong with America." After this dire diagnosis, he offered no cure except a vague wave back to the wonderful past— somehow restoring "faith in each other" by relying on "all the lessons of our heritage"—and then fired half his cabinet. Because he privately referred to America's *malaise* as he'd prepared the speech—"the President will try to transfer the wide dissatisfaction with his own performance into a 'national malaise,'" the Republican ex-speechwriter Safire previewed in his *Times* column forty-eight hours beforehand—journalists afterward named it "the malaise speech," and that stuck. The president continued with scolding jeremiads for the rest of his term, such as one about high inflation in which he reminded Americans of the "discipline" that they needed to start exercising and the "pain" and "painful steps" they'd be required to suffer.*

Americans wanted to *feel* a jolt of old-fashioned national solidarity, of the kind they remembered or imagined feeling before the late 1960s,

---

*On its editorial about this speech, *The Boston Globe* accidentally and infamously printed a joke headline—MUSH FROM THE WIMP.

not merely be reminded by Parson Carter they weren't feeling it anymore. One of the points of the 1970s pivot toward the old days was to feel happier about being Americans—*Happy Days* was the name of the TV show—because Vietnam and the rest of the 1960s had made so many people feel ambivalent or worse. Carter was unwilling or unable to indulge the manic performative patriotism that was becoming obligatory for American politicians in the 1970s.

In many senses, America's 1970s were not a repudiation but an extension of the late 1960s. The new norms and habits of mind spread and scaled, became entrenched, and no longer seemed remarkably new. Female and nonwhite people were treated more equally. The anti-Establishment subjectivity and freedom to ignore experts and believe in make-believe that exploded in the '60s was normalized and spread during the '70s and beyond. Freedoms of religion and speech continued to be exercised extravagantly. The signifiers of bohemian nonconformity—long hair, drug use, casual sex, casual clothes, rock music—became ubiquitous, standard, mainstream. A single two-year period in the mid-'70s seems like a hinge moment in this regard: the Vietnam War ended, the oldest baby boomers turned thirty, the youngest baby boomers entered puberty, *Rolling Stone* moved from a hippie dump in San Francisco to a fancy Establishment building in midtown Manhattan, the new president was a Dylan fan, *Saturday Night Live* went on the air, the Apple II was invented, and Microsoft was founded.

In retrospect, Milton Friedman's 1970 manifesto on behalf of shameless greed amounted to a preliminary offer by the philosopher-king of the economic right to forge a grand bargain with the cultural left. Both sides could find common ground concerning ultra-individualism and mistrust of government. And by the end of the 1970s, only the formalities remained to execute the agreement. Going forward, the masses would be permitted as never before to indulge their hedonistic and self-expressive impulses. And capitalists in return would also be unshackled, free to indulge their own animal spirits with fewer and fewer fetters in the forms of regulation, taxes, or social opprobrium. "Do your own thing" is not necessarily so different from "every man for himself." That could mean calling it quits on a marriage more quickly—the divorce rate doubled in the 1970s—or opting out of marriage altogether, or smoking weed, or wearing blue jeans every day, or refusing to agree to gun regulation—or rich people paying themselves as much as they wanted, or banks misleading borrowers and speculating recklessly. Deal? Deal.

So around when Tom Wolfe named it the Me Decade in 1976, the new hyperselfishness expanded beyond personal vanity and self-absorption and extreme religion to encompass the political economy as well. And indispensable to that was the one way the American sensibility definitely *changed* after the 1960s: nostalgia became a mania. With so many Americans so charmed by the cultural past in so many ways, it was easier to persuade them that restoring a version of the economic past would somehow make them happier—the past when the federal government didn't give away so much to the undeserving poor and fought wars they didn't lose.

The great political opportunity at the end of the 1970s was to play to the Me Decade's narcissism by using nostalgia—cynically, smoothly, theatrically—to cut through the despondency. A new majority of Americans were ready to be impressed by a president who convincingly and comfortingly promised to lead them into an American future resembling the American past. *Comfort* was key. Since the early 1960s, the conservatives' political harnessing of backlash against kindly liberalism had been unsmiling and scary, all ferocious contempt. That's why Barry Goldwater lost in a landslide, why George Wallace was a national pariah, why grim Richard Nixon was smart enough not even to try to make the right-wing economic case. A reframing was required. Instead of emphasizing conservative *disgust* with the *new*, somebody had to serve up delicious-looking gobs of the beautiful past.

Ronald Reagan was an ideal figure to take advantage of the moment in every conceivable way.

He didn't just talk about the good old days, he stepped right out of them, as cheerful and easy to like as his genius pal Walt Disney's make-believe Main Street USA. Reagan was an avuncular artifact of Hollywood's golden age, sixty-eight when he announced in 1979 but a very modern American kind of old, sunny and ruddy and energetic and fun, riding the horse, wearing the jeans, doing photo-op chores around his fancy California ranch.* For years he'd been popping up on TV in old movies and an old TV series he hosted, playing generic good guys and war fighters from various old days. He was *familiar,* a charismatic celebrity (like Jack Kennedy) but never such a star that voters couldn't easily accept him in this new role, an old-fashioned midcentury American TV dad who wasn't a weenie or a tool or a crook like his immediate predecessors. Long before Dad Jokes became a meme, Reagan was a chuckling virtuoso of the form who put a fun candy coating on right-wing propaganda: "The nine most terrifying words in the English language," he loved saying, "are 'I'm from the government and I'm here to help.'"

He was also a twinkly quasi-Christian, unlike his authentically Christian sermonizing predecessor. Reagan appealed to America's newly extreme and politicized Protestants, repeatedly affirming his belief in the End Times and the Second Coming. But he did that without any of his Moral Majority allies' angry nostalgia for the old days, which alienated other voters. American Protestants were undergoing their own rapid and extreme theological makeover, from about a third belonging to evangelical churches in the early 1970s to 60 percent by the mid-1980s, and he was the ideal political recruiter for binding them to the reborn party of the old-fashioned hard-core economic right.

But in addition to being in sync with the new post-1960s conditions— extreme individualism, extreme religious belief, a sweeping embrace of nostalgia—Ronald Reagan also found himself at the convergence of three longer-term historical trends. And he possessed the perfect combination of skills and temperament to take political advantage of those as well.

The first was the general national hankering for friendly familiarity and calm following the frenzied circa-1970 finale of the century of nonstop *new,* a conservative reaction that was much more about culture and psychology than economics.

The second was that the natural evolution of the political economy had reached a critical point. Forty years after the cascading flood of

---

*In addition to being the oldest president until recently, he was the first to have been divorced—just the right dash of louche to suggest that his conservatism wasn't the unpleasant old-fashioned judgmental kind.

change that gushed forth during the 1930s, the New Deal had lost its propulsive power as it widened into a big boring American reservoir on which everyone depended but lately took for granted or held in contempt. That finally gave the New Deal's enemies their chance to undo as much of it as they could. In this effort, they exploited another definitive late-1960s change. Reagan was a conservative but was so far right he came across as a renegade. "The one unifying thing about the baby boomers," a Republican strategist told a reporter back then about that younger generation, "is that they are anti-Establishment and anti-institution," and "the Reagan appeal is to people who don't go for the Establishment and for big institutions."

The third long-term historical trend was the evolution of modern media and celebrity from words to pure images. Thirty years into the TV age, show business and presidential politics became so intertwined that Americans were ready to elect a professional entertainer-in-chief. Ronald Reagan's job from the 1930s through the mid-1960s had been to perform for cameras, reciting words written by other people, so cynics are apt to look no further than that for an explanation of his subsequent political success—good-looking TV dummy, strings pulled by right-wing puppet-masters. But that's not correct.

Reagan was no intellectual, but he'd always been a cheerful, politically engaged ideologue, and by the time he ran for office, he was more fluent in political economics than most politicians. At age thirty-five, after morphing from sincere left-winger to sincere anti-Communist liberal, he continued making political ads decrying corporations' "bigger and bigger profits" and Republican tax cuts for "the higher income brackets alone," and he repeatedly got reelected president of his show business union, the Screen Actors Guild. But before he was fifty, after reading books like Hayek's libertarian manifesto *The Road to Serfdom* and giving hundreds of speeches a year as GE's $1 million–a–year traveling ambassador, he'd turned into a sincere right-winger.

Way before the liberal 1960s, Reagan was a Milton Friedmanite giving speeches about the "stultifying hand of government regulation and interference," the "little intellectual elite in a far-distant capital" that presumed to "plan our lives for us," and—remarkably right-wing—"the immorality and discrimination of the progressive tax." Then in the fall of

1964, there on NBC in prime time was the star of the weekly Western series *Death Valley Days,* but now in a suit and tie, nominally endorsing his pal Barry Goldwater—this was the half-hour ad the campaign *did* run nationwide—but in fact introducing himself to America as a political fig-ure. Because he wasn't running for anything yet, he was free to be blunt, even extreme—in favor of letting the well-to-do opt out of Social Security, declaring that "government does nothing as well . . . as the private sector," warning against Medicare as proof that "it doesn't require expropriation or confiscation of private property or business to impose socialism on a people." One week after his network TV talk, voters repudiated that ultra-conservatism decisively—for now. But with Goldwater done, the right had a *new* avatar, another horseback-riding, fifty-something southwest-erner who wasn't too stern or scary.

And when he ran for president in 1979 and 1980, Reagan suggested his administration would resemble those of beloved dead *Democrats,* fondly alluding to FDR and Truman and JFK. It was nostalgia for old he-roes and for his own younger days—probably sincere but also well played at a time when voters' own nostalgic yearnings had become all-embracing. As he ambled briskly to the presidency, Reagan's ultra-conservative agenda for the political economy was cloaked behind an old-timey, almost nonpartisan scrim.

"Extremism in defense of liberty is no vice," Barry Goldwater had famously said in his speech accepting the Republican nomination. He *owned* it and lost. As the 1980 election cycle got under way, Goldwater marveled in his diary about the normalization of the hard right since then, which was about to permit his fellow traveler to be elected president. "It is interesting to me to watch liberals, moderates and conservatives fight-ing each other to see who can come out on top the quickest against those matters that I talked so fervently and so much about in 1964"—against regulation and unions and taxes and sharing more of the wealth, against government. "Almost every one of the principles I advocated in 1964 have become the gospel of the whole spread of the spectrum of politics."

In fact, Milton Friedman thought Goldwater had self-sacrificially fought the necessary opening skirmish for the long war that he and the rest of the economic right and big business seriously launched in the 1970s and won. "I do not believe Reagan would have been elected in 1980," Friedman said during his presidency, if Goldwater had not carried out his campaign in 1964. You've got sets of political ideas and values that take a long time to develop and have an enormous momentum. It takes a long time to turn them around. Goldwater was enormously important in providing an impetus to the subsequent move away from New Deal ideas.

8

The 1970s:
Neoliberal Useful Idiots

During my first visit to Washington, D.C., in June 1972—on the very evening of the Watergate break-in, as it happened— a mod young Department of Education bureaucrat informed me over dinner that the liberal political era in America was ending. As a seventeen-year-old fresh from Nebraska looking forward to wearing my MCGOVERN FOR PRESIDENT button to a White House reception for a hundred new high school graduates with Vice President Spiro Agnew the next day, this was a shocking revelation.

The guy turned out to be right, of course. And when I started college, I saw firsthand that the youthquake and student movement and greening of America, everything I'd spent the past few years getting stoked about, was palpably, rapidly ending. The U.S. war in Vietnam was winding down and nobody was getting drafted, so fighting the Man started to seem more like a pose than an authentic passion. I was still politically liberal, but the overwhelming focus of my college years was being on the staff of *The Harvard Lampoon*. The highlight of my sophomore year was a public *Lampoon* roast of and raucous private dinner with the right-wing icon John Wayne, who arrived at our headquarters in an armored personnel carrier a year before the U.S. surrender in Vietnam. My senior year I volunteered for the

1976 presidential campaign of Democratic senator Fred Harris, an economic populist from Oklahoma whose campaign catchphrases included "The issue is privilege" and "Take the rich off welfare." He'd been the one member of the Senate to vote against confirming Lewis Powell to the Supreme Court. My senior thesis argued that more and more white-collar jobs, thanks in part to technology, were apt to become more and more proletarian, and it discussed whether workers in such professions might follow the lead of federal air traffic controllers, who'd recently unionized.

I wasn't romantic or enthusiastic about unions the way liberals used to be. The basic college-educated-liberal attitude toward unions was evolving from solidarity to indifference to suspicion, the result of a crackup at that very moment of the old New Deal political coalition. The antiwar movement and counterculture, coming right after the successful civil rights movement, had generated intense mutual contempt between the two main kinds of white Democrats, members of the working class and the expanding New Class. The televised beatings by Chicago police of protesters outside the Democratic convention in 1968—beatings encouraged by Mayor Richard Daley, the principal national white-working-class Democratic power broker—was the most spectacular early episode in the crackup. But a lesser-known instance two years later in New York City was an even more perfectly focused display of that cultural-political fissure in its early stages.

It was 1970, a cool May morning in New York City. Two months earlier a squad of young left-wing bomb-makers had accidentally blown themselves up in a Greenwich Village townhouse owned by their comrade's dad, an ad executive who'd been vacationing on St. Kitts. And in another two months *Joe,* a movie about a factory worker who hates liberals and teams up with a Manhattan ad executive to massacre hippie communards, would become a big hit. On the Monday of that week in May, National Guard troops at Kent State University in Ohio had shot thirteen students in and around an antiwar protest, killing four of them. So that Friday in lower Manhattan on Wall Street, around the statue of George Washington in front of the Federal Hall National Memorial, a thousand people, mostly students, gathered for an antiwar protest and memorial vigil. Not far away at City Hall, the American flag had been lowered to half-mast. New York police were in position around the demonstration.

Suddenly a couple of hundred union construction workers, a lot of them wearing hard hats and carrying tools, swarmed into the crowded intersection, chanting *All the way, U.S.A.* and *Love it or leave it.* "The workers, marching behind a cluster of American flags, swept policemen aside and moved on the students," according to the *Times* account. They beat up scores of protesters as well as random passersby, kicked them, bashed them with hard hats, and struck them with crowbars and pliers. The attack was organized by the leaders of the workers' union; a Wall Street executive told the *Times* he'd watched "two men in gray suits and gray hats 'directing the construction workers with hand motions.'" Then the mob moved north, where some smashed the windows of a college building and pulled down and burned a peace banner. Across the street, others burst into City Hall and raised the lowered flag. After a city official re-lowered it, angry workers bullied a deputy mayor into raising it again.

The Hard Hat Riot got extensive national press attention—as a kid in Nebraska, I watched film of it on TV and read about it in *Time.* Plastic hard hats became a nationalist antiliberal icon. And union workers in New York City kept at it, marching in the streets day after day for nearly two weeks, "vaulting police lines to chase those who raised their fingers in the 'V' peace salute." The mayor had condemned the initial riot, which made him—John Lindsay, handsome prep-school Yale WASP, a liberal Republican for whom "limousine liberal" had been coined one year earlier—a natural target for the marching workers. They carried "signs calling the mayor a rat, a commie rat, a faggot, a leftist, an idiot, a neurotic, an anarchist and a traitor," a news story reported. (The construction workers' union was already in a fight with Lindsay for his executive order requiring them to increase black and Hispanic membership.) Watching a final 100,000-person antiprotester protest march in Manhattan that had been officially organized by the union, a Brooklyn college kid told a reporter, "I'm scared. If this is what the class struggle is all about, there's something wrong."

Beginning right then, in fact, the suspicion and contempt between less-educated white people and the liberal white bourgeoisie *was* what the American class struggle was most visibly and consciously about. And it would define our politics as the economy was reshaped to do better than ever for yuppies and worse and worse for the proles, regardless of their ideologies and cultural tastes.

During the 1960s, liberals had started falling out of love with unions for reasons more directly related to the political economy. It was another side effect of triumphalist liberal complacency, how Americans in general were taking for granted the progress and prosperity that the New Deal had helped make possible. Sure, back in the day unions had been an essential countervailing force to business, but now—having won forty-hour weeks, good healthcare, good pensions, autoworker salaries of $75,000 (in 2020 dollars), OSHA, the EEOC—organized labor was victorious, powerful, the Establishment. "These powerful institutions," the former machinist Irving Kristol astutely wrote at the beginning of 1970, just before publicly moving full right, were "inexorably being drained of meaning, and therefore of legitimacy." As a result, "trade unionism has become that most dangerous of social phenomena: a boring topic," and "none of the younger reporters is interested in spending so much time in the company of trade union officials."

Apart from organized labor's apparently permanent hold on decisive power at the time, another reason people like me found unions kind of boring was that a unionized job was almost by definition a boring job. When I started work as a writer at *Time* in 1981, I joined the union, the Newspaper Guild, but I understood that everything I cared about in that job—good assignments, decent salary increases, titular honorifics— would be entirely at my editors' discretion, not a function of union rules.* A union? Sure, fine. But I was *talent*. I was *creative*. I was an *individual*.† College graduates tend to want to think of themselves that way, younger ones all the more, younger ones starting with baby boomers the most. And the intensified, all-encompassing individualism that blew up during the 1960s and then continued—*I do my thing, and you do your thing. I am not in this world to live up to your expectations*—wasn't a mindset or temperament that necessarily reinforced feelings of solidarity with fellow workers or romantic feelings about unions.

---

*A bumbling, ineffectual strike by Time Inc.'s one thousand editorial employees, the first ever, had taken place a few years before I got there; its big demand had been that raises be exactly the same for everyone in percentage terms. After editors and managers successfully produced the next issues of the monthlies and three issues of the weeklies on schedule, the strikers gave up. The big problem, according to the head of *Time*'s Newspaper Guild, was the "large number of members new to the idea of a union, let alone a strike."
†I've been an enthusiastic dues-paying and voting member of the Writers Guild, the union for TV and film writers, for three decades.

What happened with organized labor in journalism during the 1970s is an excellent illustration of those early days of the deepening, widening fracture between upper-middle-class and lower-middle-class (white) Americans. It encompasses both the cultural split, yuppies versus yahoos, and the introduction of transformative technology in the workplace.

Between the publication of the Pentagon Papers in 1971 and the end of Watergate in 1974, *The Washington Post* became a celebrated national institution, sexy liberalism incarnate. Following immediately on those two heroic achievements was another milestone episode, neither very celebrated nor heroic but likewise emblematic of the moment. In the spring of 1974, the journalists of the *Post* went out on strike—bumblingly. They didn't even ask the paper's blue-collar unions to join them, they refused their own Newspaper Guild leaders' request to walk a picket line, the paper continued publishing, and after two weeks they gave up and accepted management's offer.

It was a generation before websites and browsers, universal PCs and cellphones, thirty years before print dailies entered their death spiral, but technology was already changing newspapers in a big way— the *manufacturing* part of the operation. Owners were eliminating typographers, who operated obsolete, elephantine *Brazil*–meets–*Willie Wonka* Linotype machines that turned molten lead into blocks of type, and they also wanted to pay fewer workers to operate the printing presses. A large majority of the *Post*'s two thousand employees were those blue-collar guys, and a large majority of them were suddenly redundant. In 1975 the two hundred pressmen wouldn't come to terms and went on strike, and the other blue-collar unions at the *Post* went on strike in solidarity, as unions are supposed to do. On their way out, some of the pressmen sabotaged some of the presses, a major strategic error. Quite a few of the nonunion strikebreakers whom management hired to replace the (white) strikers were black, a brilliant strategic decision.

And absolutely key to how it played out was the behavior of the *Post*'s journalists. Just as the recent exposure of the secret Pentagon report on Vietnam and Nixon's crimes had been game-changing work by journalists with the essential support of management, the crushing of the strike and pressmen's union, also game-changing, was the work of management with the essential support of journalists.

Two-thirds of the *Post's* unionized editorial employees didn't stop working at all, and a majority voted again and again against striking in solidarity with the pressmen. "What I find ominous is that a number of Guild people don't think they have common cause with craftsmen," a *Post* journalist told a reporter at the time. "They feel professionally superior to guys with dirt under their fingernails." At a guild meeting, a *Post* reporter referred to the striking pressmen as "slack-jawed cretins." Four weeks into the five-month strike, a *Times* article reported that "if a *Post* Guild member is asked why he or she is not supporting the strike," many "say they do not see themselves as ordinary working people. One said, 'We go to the same parties as management. We know Kissinger, too.'" And while probably none of the pressmen knew the secretary of state, their average pay was the equivalent of $111,000, about as much as reporters, which is the excuse one of the paper's reporters gave for crossing the picket line from day one. "If they got slave wages, I'd be out on the line myself," said thirty-two-year-old Bob Woodward, co-author of the second-best-selling nonfiction book of the previous year.

The strike ended just before the release of the film adaptation of *All the President's Men,* a fictionalization that only intensified the love of American liberals and journalists for *The Washington Post,* even though the *Post* press-room was about to become nonunion and membership in the journalists' union, the Guild, strictly optional. As a *Post* columnist wrote back then in *The New Republic,* "The pressmen's strike was crushed with methods and with a severity that the press in general or the *Post* in particular would not be likely to regard as acceptable from the owners of steel mills. Yet because it was a newspaper management that broke the strike, no other newspaper has touched it properly, or even whimpered a protest."

When I arrived at *Time* a few years later, I went out of my way to produce copy the *modern* way—abandoning my office Selectric to use one of the special computer terminals crammed into a special little room, holed up with a few of the other young writers. That technology presently enabled the company to eliminate the jobs of the people downstairs who were employed to retype our stories. At the time I probably shrugged, like the newspaper reporters who hadn't cared much about the redundant Linotype operators and pressmen.

If I'd been one of those unionized craft workers who were abandoned by my unionized journalist colleagues forty-five years ago, I think that during these last fifteen years, watching journalists get washed away and drowned by the latest wave of technology-induced change, I'd have felt some schadenfreude.

It's a close-to-home example of that spiral of mistrust and resentment that wasn't only cultural, hard hats versus hippies, but about earning a living, the changing political economy. And what happened at newspapers (and magazines) back then also had disproportionate impact on this whole history because once journalists were actively ambivalent about organized labor, that disenchantment spread more contagiously than if it had just been random young professionals disrespecting and bad-mouthing unions. News stories about labor now tended to be framed *this* way rather than *that* way or were not covered at all. Thus, like Democratic politicians in Washington at the same time, media people became enablers of the national change in perspective from left to right concerning economics.

I'm not claiming that labor unions are always virtuous or aren't frequently annoying. Parochial, shortsighted, and other kinds of misguided, with a rich history of racism, sexism, and corruption—construct your own critique. I heard every criticism growing up as the opposite of a red-diaper baby; my father was a lawyer whose practice was negotiating with unions on behalf of employers.

But they or equivalent vehicles must exist and have serious power. It's a question of achieving a decent balance, a dynamic tension and equilibrium among the various players in the political economy—workers and employers and citizens. The balance this country managed from the 1930s through the 1970s worked and seemed fair. Then over the last few decades, as unions and belief in the premise of organized labor weakened, big business and the wealthy took predatory advantage, and the system became highly unbalanced. It's important to look hard at how liberals were variously complacent and complicit as that unbalancing happened.

During the 1930s and '40s and '50s, the right had derided liberal writers and editors as Communists' "useful idiots," doing soft propaganda work for the extreme left; it looks in retrospect as if starting in the 1970s, a lot of them—of us—became capitalists' useful idiots. Indeed, that's how the former socialist Kristol foresaw the huge new cohort of college-educated liberal professionals being co-opted into the system. "A good part of this process of assimilation," he advised conservatives and capitalists in the

1970s, "will be the education of this 'new class' in the actualities of business and economics—*not* their conversion to 'free enterprise'—so that they can exercise power responsibly. It will be an immense educational task, in which the business community can certainly play an important role."

During the 1960s, the decade of maximum new here in our land of the new, the New Deal had started to seem old, one more thing over thirty not to trust. The institutionalized political left that had grown out of that era was renamed the Old Left, because the younger generation—in some cases more radical, in all cases groovier—was called the New Left. As I've said, at the moment the revolution failed and voters rejected McGovernite ultra-liberalism, Americans of every caste were giving themselves over to romanticizing the past in pop culture and high art. The smart sets were reviving and recycling old forms and styles, not just returning decoration to architecture but melody to classical music and human figures to fine art—all of which felt charmingly old but also unfamiliar, fresh, excitingly . . . new.

In politics and public policy too, the past was being selectively rediscovered. Fancy-college-educated liberals, who like artists and cultural gatekeepers still defined themselves by their openness to the new and challenging, chose not to return to the tired FDR liberalism of the older generations with whom they'd been fighting an internecine war for a decade. Rather, the unfamiliar things they dusted off were pieces of the old conservative critique of New Deal liberalism—which was a bit transgressive, therefore cool. They became the New Democrats, as opposed to the old New Deal Democrats, the *new* new versus the old new.

Fred Dutton was a prominent professional Democrat who'd worked in the Kennedy White House, then for Vice President Humphrey, then for Bobby Kennedy's presidential campaign in 1968. In the summer of 1971, this middle-aged Establishment liberal published a very ahead-of-the-curve book called *Changing Sources of Power* that predicted and advocated for a new species of liberalism geared toward white-collar workers and especially youth. He praised the baby boomers for providing "a severe psychic jolt for traditional liberals, who long ago came to believe that they had an almost exclusive stewardship over the American conscience." In the 1970s, he said, "the greatest shift is the current tipping of the balance of politi-

cal power from the economic to the psychological, from the stomach and
pocketbook to the psyche." In other words, more or less: forget political
economics, forget the blue-collar guys, forget unions, it's all about the college kids, we're entering the Me Decade.

One afternoon that same summer, 1971, at age sixteen, I was
among 100 or 150 people in Omaha's big central park watching Senator George McGovern deliver a speech. He was the most liberal, most
antiwar candidate for the Democratic nomination. I remember nothing of what he said, because I was furtively inching toward and trying
to overhear the two men standing near me: thirty-four-year-old Warren Beatty and McGovern's thirty-four-year-old campaign director,
Gary Hart, who I also recognized because I was a politics geek and a
McGovern volunteer.

McGovern had led the Democratic Party commission that had just
democratized the process of nominating presidential candidates, making
it a matter of winning citizens' votes in primaries and public caucuses
rather than delegates' votes at closed party conventions. Which meant
that from then on it was much harder for labor unions to influence the
Democrats' choice of nominee—which in turn enabled Hart to help win
the 1972 nomination for the hippie-loving antiwar women's lib acid amnesty abortion candidate whom the blue-collar union members tended to
despise.

Immediately after the 1972 wipeout, Hart launched his own first
political candidacy, for a U.S. Senate seat in Colorado. The Vietnam
War and its cultural waves had made leaders and members of unions
dislike McGovern, but as a child of the Depression and former history professor, he had totally been on their side concerning the whole
point of unions—maximizing worker power versus corporate power in
the economy. Hart, on the other hand, was at odds with the working
class on both counts, a cool young Yalie who barely pretended to be
their economic ally.

"We are not a bunch of little Hubert Humphreys," he said during
his 1974 Senate campaign, referring to his party's 1968 presidential
candidate, whom McGovern had beaten for the nomination in 1972.
Vice President Humphrey had epitomized the compromised passé liberalism hated by the New Left for supporting the Vietnam War, so Hart
was playing to that accumulated ill will. But in fact, ideologically, he

had jumped overnight from the left of Humphrey and company to their right.

Hart's 1974 Senate campaign stump speech was actually called "The End of the New Deal." He disparaged liberals who thought that "if there is a problem, [you] create an agency and throw money at the problem," who "clung to the Roosevelt model long after it ceased to relate to reality"—and to that he added some sexist shade, calling them "the Eleanor Roosevelt wing" of the party. "The ballyhooed War on Poverty" of the 1960s, the Democratic programs that included Medicaid and food stamps, "succeeded only in raising the expectations, but not the living conditions, of the poor," he said inaccurately. "This nation desperately needs a new breed of thinkers and doers who will question old premises and disregard old alliances." In that first post-Watergate election, Hart beat the Republican incumbent by a landslide and became the very model of a modern major Democrat.

I felt an affinity for this new, youthy, college-educated political wing—as I felt at the time for postmodern architecture and New Wave music. I was in my twenties, so partly it was the sheer hubris of the young, rejecting the older generation because it was old. Hart's Senate campaign slogan was "They had their turn. Now it's our turn."

But more than that, I actually, earnestly considered myself a new breed of thinker questioning old premises and disregarding old alliances. I wanted to be counterintuitive, contrarian, evidence-based, ready to look at everything afresh. Like so many in my generation, I learned from the war in Vietnam and the war on drugs to mistrust the government, so maybe in other ways it had gotten bloated and inefficient, maybe nitpicky regulations were making it too hard to do business, maybe the antitrust approach invented in my great-grandparents' day was outmoded. And weren't labor unions retrograde and lumbering in lots of ways? Why, for instance, couldn't we imagine *new* forms of worker solidarity and security? In the late 1970s, when the government was about to bail out Chrysler and a freshman Democratic senator, Paul Tsongas, proposed guaranteeing the workers $1.1 billion in the form of Chrysler stock rather than wage increases, why didn't that make sense?

And thus a new buzzword that spread like mad during the 1970s and '80s through art and culture, *postmodernism*, acquired a younger sibling

in American politics—*neoliberalism.* Back in the 1970s and '80s, at least
in the United States, neoliberalism wasn't yet what it is in the twenty-
first century, leftists' all-encompassing derogatory term for anything to the
right of nationalized-industry socialism.* Rather, it was a term proudly
self-applied by a certain kind of wonk. Their wellspring was an intensely
reportorial little magazine called *The Washington Monthly* founded in
1969 and run by a cofounder of the Peace Corps, Charlie Peters. It had
a circulation of less than 40,000 in the 1970s and early '80s when I sub-
scribed, but during that pivotal political period, it had an outsize influence in reshaping center-left thought and policy.†

All enlightened, open-minded people should "distrust *all* automatic responses, liberal or conservative," Peters said—and who could
disagree?—so "the liberal movement has to change and reject the liberal
clichés and automatic responses of the past," such as "their old habits
of automatically favoring unions and opposing business." There was too
much loyalty to the ideological home team, which followed the rules of
"Don't say anything bad about the good guys" because "any criticism is
only likely to strengthen the hand of their enemies," and "Don't say anything good about the bad guys." Peters's new tendency consisted of "liberals who decided to retain their old goals while abandoning the prejudices
that they realized were blinding them to the real nature of many of the nation's problems" that had begun "to cripple the nation"—such as declining productivity and "decaying plants and infrastructure" and "inefficient
and unaccountable public agencies." The notion, certainly among many
writers and thinkers if not necessarily the politicians, wasn't to pursue
centrism or moderation for their own sakes, or cynical political triangula-
tion between left and right, but intellectual rigor and honesty.

---

*There's a long etymology here. In the 1930s, when anti–New Deal economic libertarians
were called liberals, as they still are outside the United States, some became known as
"neoliberals." By the 1970s the term was occasionally used to describe the radical New
Left, then the wonky-moderate-Democrat self-definition came and went, supplanted
around 2000 by today's expansive everyone-from-Milton-Friedman-to-Elizabeth-Warren
meaning.
†Outsize influence then and now: a quorum of its writers and editors from the early days
remain big-deal journalists and commentators, including Jonathan Alter, James Fallows,
David Ignatius, Mickey Kaus, Michael Kinsley, Nicholas Lemann, Joe Nocera, and Walter Shapiro. Other prominent staff from later years include Katherine Boo, Nick Con-
fessore, Gregg Easterbrook, Suzannah Lessard, Josh Marshall, Jon Meacham, Timothy
Noah, Nicholas Thompson, Steven Waldman, and Benjamin Wallace-Wells.

The new approach propagated rapidly. The young *Washington Monthly* writer-editor Michael Kinsley took over the main weekly magazine of Washington liberalism, *The New Republic,* and the young *Washington Monthly* writer-editor Jim Fallows became one of President Carter's speechwriters. "There is a legitimate modesty now about intervening in the economy," said the young head of antitrust enforcement in the Carter Justice Department. "The hard-bitten D.A. approach isn't very useful and the people in Justice recognize that."* Soon almost every up-and-coming national Democratic politician was a New Democrat: Hart, Tsongas, Jerry Brown, Bill Bradley, Al Gore, Bob Kerrey, Bill Clinton—all first elected senator or governor between 1974 and 1984 when they were in their thirties, all about to become serious presidential candidates.

For two generations, liberals had been in control of the government *and* the news media *and* the culture, so it seemed as if that hegemony afforded them the luxury of true liberalism—admitting mistakes, cutting some slack for the other side, trying new approaches. For forty-four of the previous forty-eight years Democrats had controlled both houses of Congress, and they had also held the presidency for most of that half-century. The Harvard professor Daniel Moynihan, for instance, served in four straight administrations, two Democratic and two Republican, before becoming an unpredictable Democratic senator from New York in 1977. All through the 1970s, when the GOP had only about a third of Senate seats, a third of those Republicans were bona fide liberals. *Of course* good-faith compromise and consensus between left and right were possible.

At the end of the 1970s, liberal PBS commissioned a ten-episode Friday-night series starring Milton Friedman called *Free to Choose.* Its funders included General Motors, General Mills, and PepsiCo. The executive producer said the show, *airing on the Public Broadcasting Service,* would explain to viewers like you "how we've become puppets of big government." On the show, Friedman explained why federal taxes, the Food and Drug Administration, public schools, and labor unions, among other bêtes noires, were bad for America. "The economic controls that have

---

*As it happened, his antitrust experience had been entirely in private practice, representing corporations, as an attorney at the law firm of Lewis Powell before and after he wrote the Powell Memo and became a Supreme Court justice.

proliferated in the United States in recent decades," his accompanying bestselling book asserted, "have also affected our freedom of speech, of press, and of religion." Conveniently for the right, the series premiered in early January 1980, just before the first primary elections in which Reagan was one of many major Republican candidates.

But despite the liberal Establishment's openness and the right's new think tanks and foundations and zillionaire donors, it seemed in the 1970s that the antigovernment diehards and libertarian freaks, the Milton Friedmanites and Ayn Randians and *Wall Street Journal* ideologues, would never *really* be allowed to run the show. The American ideological center of gravity was plainly undergoing a rightward shift, but wouldn't the 1980s just turn out to be some kind of modest course correction, like what happened in the late 1940s and '50s, part of the normal endless back-and-forth pendulum swing from center-left to center-right?

We had no idea. Almost nobody foresaw fully the enormity of the sharp turn America was about to take. Nobody knew that we'd keep heading in that direction for half a lifetime, that in the late 1970s big business and the well-to-do were at the start of a forty-year-plus winning streak at the expense of everyone else.

Partly as a result of various kinds of liberal *niceness,* liberals were ill-prepared to appreciate or cope with what was about to happen. The energized economic right was led by corporations and the rich as well as zealots who'd been shut out of real power for decades—whereas liberals found zealotry vulgar and, although they'd been broadly empowered for decades, didn't have big money riding on the outcome. The New Democrats were more like journalists and academics than traditional political types, more inclined to be polite than tough. Modern liberals prided ourselves on *not* being ideologues, on entertaining all sorts of disparate policy ideas for improving the world, whereas the economic right really has one big, simple idea—do everything possible to let the rich stay rich and get richer.

That last difference is the crucial one. Most Americans, even those to the left, have been reluctant to subscribe fully to Marx's basic big idea, that modern society is shaped by an endless struggle between capital and labor, owners and workers, the rich and powerful versus everyone else. Our special American reluctance to go there has several different sources. We've never been a classless society, of course, but at the start we were a lot closer than most of the rest of the world. In 1830 the richest 1 percent of Americans received less than 10 percent of all the income, just half the share taken by Britain's richest 1 percent at the time.* Slavery made factory owners look good compared to Southern plantation owners, and we fought a war to prove the point. The American Dream, in which a plucky individual moved up in the world and even turned from a worker into a boss, actually came true often enough to make people believe it might happen to them. For most of a century, the Soviet Union and the other countries that called themselves Marxist were terrible advertisements for anything from that lineage. For a long time, Americans did a good job using the government and other means—persuasion, threats, shame, honor—to level up workers' and citizens' shares of money and power, and to limit the shares taken by big business and the rich. As the wealth was distributed more equally, it grew faster than ever, which also disinclined most people to think of America as a place run by a minority of greedy, cheating self-dealers at the expense of a large majority.

So most liberals, like most Americans, preferred not to regard capitalists as categorically rapacious and amoral, or to imagine the U.S. political economy as a never-ending class war in which everyone must ultimately choose between two sides. That seemed crude. They didn't vote for Reagan, but most didn't *hate* him, certainly not at first, because in their way they shared his dreamy faith in the 1940s Frank Capra movie vision of America. It was during the 1970s that *It's a Wonderful Life* was rediscovered and made an icon—by liberals. And to some degree, most succumbed, like most Americans, to a new form of economic nostalgia that was being revived and popularized—the notion that market forces are practically natural forces with which we dare not tinker or tamper too much. Finally, upper-middle-class liberals didn't want to think badly of all their friends and neighbors and classmates who happened to work at banks or in real estate or the vicinity of C-suites.

Starting in the 1970s, the Friedman Doctrine and its extrapolations freed and encouraged businesspeople and the rich to go ahead and conform to the left-wing caricatures of them, to be rapacious and amoral

---

* By the end of the 1970s, we'd gotten the 1 percent's share back down to that egalitarian early American level, but since then it has more than doubled, so U.S. economic unfairness in 2020 is similar to British economic unfairness in 1830.

without shame. Indeed, the new economic right even encouraged them to wage class war—explicitly against the affluent "New Class" of (traitorous white) liberal professionals and the (black) "underclass," more discretely against the (white) working class they were enlisting as political allies. Meanwhile liberals clung to their strong preference to see both sides, meet halfway, seem reasonable. Such a colossal irony: after socialists and Communists in the 1930s and then the New Left in the 1960s had tried and failed to achieve a radical class-based reordering of the American political economy, the economic far right took its shot at doing that in the 1970s and succeeded beyond anyone's wildest hope or fear.

electricity—the big businesses that were taking over the industry saw an opportunity. They got Washington, in full deregulation mania, to radically deregulate their booming industry—specifically, to make it *illegal* for local authorities to regulate the fees the local cable monopolists could charge local citizens. The Senate passed the bill 87–9, the House on a voice vote, and Reagan signed it into law a week before his landslide reelection in 1984.

Right away the cable operators did what monopolists do: in the first four years after deregulation took effect, the average cost of the most basic cable service rose 61 percent. A generation later, the lucky big businesses that had come to control cable service started offering fast access to the Web as well, making them even luckier—virtually unregulated quasi-monopolists selling one highly desirable utility, TV, and a second, genuinely essential utility, the Internet.

At least cable TV and the Internet were actually new technologies that required us to figure out new ways of regulating them—or, as it happened, declining to regulate them. By contrast, no technological breakthroughs occurred in the 1980s that obliged the government to allow pharmaceutical companies to deluge American citizens with ads for prescription medicines. Rather, two industries consisting of very big businesses, pharma and media, took advantage of free-market mania.

In this case, they took us back in time to the turn of the twentieth century, before Americans decided it wasn't a good idea to let makers of medicines that were unnecessary or dangerous advertise them freely, back when half of newspapers' ad income came from bogus and/or addictive patent medicines. From 1906 to 1962, federal law regulated medicines ever more closely, trying to make sure they were safe and did what they were supposed to do. As new pharmaceuticals proliferated, a federal law in 1951 finally established the legal category of prescription-only drugs. In the industry, they were known as "ethical pharmaceuticals" and "ethical drugs."

And the industry quite effectively self-regulated, ethically, marketing those drugs exclusively to physicians . . . until the 1980s. There was no federal law against advertising prescription drugs directly to consumers in newspapers and magazines and on TV, just sensible norms, observed all over the world, that it was a bad idea. But then in the early 1980s, a couple of pharmaceutical companies began running a few ads

on TV, and the FDA asked them to stop, pretty please, for a moratorium. Then in 1985 it lifted the moratorium. Ads on TV popped up, at
first without actually naming the drugs, then naming them, then pushing the boundaries more. Pharma quickly became, so to speak, addicted
to consumer advertising, as did, of course, advertising-supported media,
especially TV networks, which had spent the 1980s encouraging the drug
companies to begin consumer advertising and the Republican administrations to give it a green light. After an FDA commissioner tried to hold
back the tide, the Republican Speaker of the House, Newt Gingrich,
called the agency America's "number one job killer," and the floodgates
opened wide. Suddenly in the 1990s such ads were all over the place.
In 1991 the pharmaceutical industry's total consumer ad spending was
$102 million in today's dollars, a small fraction of it going to television;
just seven years later it was twenty times higher, more than $2 billion,
$1 billion of that on TV. Since then pharmaceutical ad spending has tri-
pled to more than $6 billion a year.

For the pharmaceutical as well as the media business, allowing consumer ads for prescription drugs, a deregulation that required no laws being debated or passed or repealed, worked splendidly. In 1980 the average
American spent the same on prescription drugs as she had in 1970. By
1990 that amount had doubled, then it doubled again before the end of
the decade, and since then it has more than doubled again. So we now
spend *ten times* on prescription drugs, in real dollars, what we spent in
1970—and not just because drugs are much more expensive, thanks to
all the micro-monopolies our big-business-friendly government creates
for individual drugs. We see the ads, so we simply take lots more, surely
more than we need and more than is healthy. America is exceptional, in
this as in so many ways. Only one other country on Earth, New Zealand,
allows prescription drugs to be advertised directly to its citizens.* Until
the 1990s, we spent around the same per person on prescription drugs
as Canadians and western Europeans, but now we spend as much as 200
percent more. By the way, after the 1980s the term *ethical drug* quickly
faded from use. That was probably just a coincidence.

---

*In 2015 the doctors' American Medical Association finally declared itself in favor of a
federal ban on mass-market prescription drug advertising.

13

The Culture of Greed Is Good

T he public face of American business, in the middle of the
twentieth century, was reliable, responsible, deliberately boring. In fiction, Ayn Rand, especially in *Atlas Shrugged* (1957),
depicted big businessmen as fuck-you swashbucklers, but the real ones
didn't dare come off like that. As late as 1981, when left-wing professor Marshall Berman finished writing *All That Is Solid Melts into Air*,
he noted how reticent corporate leaders were, seldom celebrating the
intrinsic thrills and chills of capitalism. How ironic, he wrote, that in
this modern CEOs, obliged to appear to be reassuring *anti*radicals, had
been outdone a century earlier by Karl Marx's enthusiastic depiction of
capitalism's "revolutionary energy and audacity, its dynamic creativity,
its adventurousness and romance, its capacity to make men not merely
more comfortable but more alive." As Berman said of modern American
corporate executives:

> Even as they frighten everyone with fantasies of proletarian rapac-
> ity and revenge, they themselves, through their inexhaustible deal-
> ing and developing, hurtle masses of men, materials and money
> up and down the earth, and erode or explode the foundations of
> everyone's lives as they go. Their secret—a secret they have man-

aged to keep even from themselves—is that behind their facades, they are the most violently destructive ruling class in history.

But in fact, after working up to it for a decade, America's capitalists were finally, fully *feeling* the destructive glee and at that very moment coming out of the closet, loud and proud. It's remarkable how well in 1987 a big Hollywood movie—a movie distributed by the studio Rupert Murdoch had recently acquired—dramatized, in real time, the unashamed new money-money-money American zeitgeist that considered capitalism nothing but *awesome*. It wouldn't and couldn't have been made just a dozen years earlier.

The main plot points of Oliver Stone's *Wall Street* were spot on: a superstar financial speculator engages in illegal inside trading, a predatory takeover strips a profitable company of its assets, and unionized workers are bamboozled into going along with a deal that will leave them without their good jobs and pensions. The corporate raider Gordon Gekko, played by Michael Douglas, does get his comeuppance in the end because his stockbroker, the Charlie Sheen character who provided him with the tradable inside information about his mechanic father's airline company, flips on him. But Gekko is the star of the show, the exciting sexy late-model 1980s antihero.

The most memorable scene from *Wall Street* is Gekko's speech to a meeting in a big hotel ballroom in midtown Manhattan of hundreds of shareholders of a paper manufacturer in which he's bought up stock to execute a hostile takeover. The company's stuffy old CEO speaks first, explaining to his investors that he is "fighting the get-rich-quick, short-term-profit, slot-machine mentality of Wall Street." In this new approach to American business, "we are undermining our foundation. This cancer is called *greed*. Greed and speculation have replaced long-term investment. Corporations are being taken apart like Erector Sets, without any consideration of the public good."

Then the smirking, charismatic, sharply dressed Gekko strides onto the podium. "We're not here to indulge in *fantasy*," he says, "but in political and economic *reality*." Then he harks back nostalgically to the good old days of the nineteenth and early twentieth centuries, as the real-life capitalist right actually did and does—

the days of the free market, when our country was a top industrial power, there was accountability to the stockholder. The Carnegies, the Mellons, the men that built this great industrial empire, made sure of it because it was *their money* at stake. . . . You own the company. That's right—*you*, the stockholder. And you are all being royally screwed over by these, these *bureaucrats*. . . . The new law of evolution in corporate America seems to be survival of the *un*-fittest. . . . I am not a destroyer of companies. I am a *liberator* of them. The point is, ladies and gentlemen, that *greed*—for lack of a better word—is *good*. Greed is *right*. Greed *works*. Greed clarifies, cuts through, and captures the essence of the evolutionary spirit. . . . And *greed*—you mark my words—will not only save Teldar Paper, but that other malfunctioning corporation called the USA!

In just four minutes, Gekko summarized and incarnated the U.S. political economy's new doctrine. It was Libertarian Economics for Dummies, the Friedman Doctrine dramatized, a stump speech for money and its manipulation as the root of all glory.

And in the movie, Gekko's audience responds with wild applause, a standing ovation, the whole crowd ecstatic over his endorsement of single-minded financial marauding. And life imitated art, which was imitating life. Among the millions of Americans watching in theaters and at home on TV were tens or hundreds of thousands of actual and would-be investors and traders and bankers and bloody-minded players of the system who were electrified and inspired, virtually coked up. I've met business guys who can recite Gekko's lines. For them, it was a rousing band-of-brothers speech to the assembled mercenaries in the new war. The Gekko character's commission of felonies was almost incidental, part of the plot because a Hollywood movie requires them, although the crimes also make him seem even more badass.

Lots of *Wall Street* fans also got their ferocious animal spirits ignited by watching and memorizing the most memorable scene from a contemporaneous companion piece, David Mamet's *Glengarry Glen Ross*, where Alec Baldwin's character Blake mysteriously arrives to terrify an office of real estate salesmen. "A-B-C—A, always, *B*, be, *C*, closing. *Always be closing*," "Coffee's for closers only," "Do you think I'm fucking with you? I am *not* fucking

with you," "Nice guy? I don't give a shit. Good father? Fuck you, go home and play with your kids," and "What's my name? *Fuck You,* that's my name."*
He's like a hellish noncommissioned officer to Gekko's gleefully demonic general in the U.S. capitalist legion as it was then being reconstituted.

In 1987 as well, some Wall Street guys started referring to themselves as Masters of the Universe, thanks to *The Bonfire of the Vanities,* Tom Wolfe's novel inspired, as he said, by "the ambitious young men (there were no women) who, starting with the 1980s, began racking up millions every year—millions!—in performance bonuses at investment banks."

Suddenly in the 1980s the news media were also celebrating and glorifying real-life big businessmen as they hadn't since the 1950s and early '60s—in fact, as they really hadn't since the 1910s and '20s. It was in 1982 that *Forbes* realized it was now acceptable to create an annual ranked list of the four hundred richest people, with estimates of their wealth, and in 1984 some A-list journalists launched a very glossy, stylish national monthly about businesspeople called *Manhattan, inc.*

The most celebrated and glorified were the megalomaniacal loud-mouth alpha-male SOBs like Lee Iacocca and Jack Welch, leaders of two of the biggest public companies, Chrysler and General Electric, who barked and swaggered in ways that such leaders hadn't really been allowed to do in the modern age. They were hired managers performing the roles of lovably tough and cantankerous founder-owners. Both companies were big old-fashioned manufacturers from the golden age, each the tenth-largest company in America when Iacocca and Welch took them over in 1979 and 1981, respectively, just as we began realizing we'd entered the twilight of big old-fashioned American manufacturing. Each is a good case study illustrating the breakneck remaking of our political economy, in response to both new technology and globalization, and by decisions that the bosses and financiers and political leaders chose to make.

In the 1970s the U.S. auto industry had responded slowly to ramped-

---

*An *Evil Geniuses*–themed film festival would include *Wall Street* (1987), *Glengarry Glen Ross* (1992), *The American President* (starring Michael Douglas, 1995), *30 Rock*'s season 4 episode 14 (in which NBC's actual ex-overlord Jack Welch plays himself with Alec Baldwin's fictional NBC executive, 2010), and Baldwin's best several *SNL* performances as Donald Trump (2016–20).

up foreign competition and higher oil prices. Chrysler did worst of all, continuing to manufacture nothing but hulking, unreliable gas-guzzlers on which it lost the equivalent of $1,000 per car. But the company was deemed too big to fail, the first, so Iacocca arranged for a nonbankruptcy bankruptcy, getting the federal government to cosign for billions in bank loans. Meanwhile, he made himself the star of Chrysler TV ads and even flirted with a presidential candidacy in 1988—his campaign slogan was to be "I Like I."

In a 1985 cover profile I wrote for *Time*, I said he was "overbearing," had "a Daffy Duck lisp," and went "hardly a half-minute without mentioning '*guys*'—specific guys or guys in the abstract, guys who build automobiles ('car guys') or sell automobiles or buy them." But I kind of liked him. In our interviews, he slagged Reagan's economic right-wingism.

> The Democrats today are more pragmatic, not so ideological. . . . We are deindustrializing the country. . . . I'm not very popular with the people around the White House anymore. I told them [on trade policy], "Let's make sure we don't get hosed." They don't like that. This Administration sees you either as a protectionist or a free-trader, with no shades in between. And we're going to lose, as a country, for it. . . . Where's Dave Stockman? Every time he tells the truth he gets in trouble. He gives them the hard facts. . . . So who's in charge of economic policy? Who are these people?

Iacocca convinced his unionized workers to agree to be paid the equivalent of $20,000 a year less than GM's and Ford's workers—and then spent the remainder of the 1980s laying half of them off. After retiring in 1992, he returned a few years later as part of a Gekko-like raider's attempted leveraged buyout of Chrysler, which failed and wound up enabling its takeover by a foreign company.*

General Electric, for its part, wasn't in trouble when Welch became CEO. Rather, Welch took advantage of the new rules of the economy to make the company's stock price skyrocket, which had been deemed,

---

*In the early twenty-first century, as the fantasy-industrial complex continued annexing American life beyond show business, Chrysler hired the eighty-year-old former CEO to be its Colonel Sanders, playing himself in TV ads with Snoop Dogg.

even more than actual profit, the only thing that matters. Like Gekko in *Wall Street* and Blake in *Glengarry*, Welch was known for being brutally candid. In fact, GE made a doctrine out of brutality, codified it as a system that ensured worker insecurity by constantly identifying a quota of doomed losers. Every year, according to Welch's new rule, one out of every ten GE employees were fired, no matter what, because nine other employees were judged by their superiors to be superior. It was called the Vitality Curve, and other big companies were soon instituting dread-inducing worker-culling systems with their own euphemistic names— Personal Business Commitments at IBM, Individual Dignity Entitlement at Motorola. At GE, many were never replaced; during Welch's first five years as CEO, the workforce shrank by a quarter, and he became known as Neutron Jack—ha!—because like a neutron bomb, he evaporated tens of thousands of people without damaging the businesses where they worked. Such corporate "rank-and-yank" systems were just one way that an acute new sense of economic insecurity spiked in the 1980s and then stayed high.

Welch also started turning GE from a manufacturing company into more of a financial services company—just as the abstract and increasingly exotic games of pure financial betting, lending, and otherwise making money by fiddling with money and hypothetical money was sucking up more of America's resources and focus and giving Wall Street ever more influence and control of our economy. In addition to eliminating jobs, the original great American technology company drastically cut back its spending on research and development. As a result, GE's profits increased (for a while) and its stock price went up phenomenally (for a while), and Jack Welch became the superstarriest CEO, worshipfully covered by the media and emulated by corporate executives. He and Iacocca and were both perfectly cast for the hypernostalgic *USA! USA!* moment—John Waynes in suits and ties, straight-talking manly men from working-class families who'd come to the rescue of enervated, simpering corporate America, taking over iconic companies to remake them for a hard-assed new age.

By the way, although American spectators had started doing that "*USA! USA!*" chant with its cheerfully fuck-you edge at international sporting events during the 1970s, it was in the 1980s that it became a national cultural habit, first at the 1980 Winter Olympics in Lake Placid, when Team USA (a new coinage) beat the unbeatable Soviet hockey team, then spreading into professional wrestling and Reagan reelection campaign rallies and finally to any sort of excited mob of Americans who felt like madly *insisting* on our awesomeness, to *perform* feelings of patriotic self-confidence, which used to abide more organically and implicitly. In other words, the *"USA! USA!"* chant was yet another expression of the nostalgia tic, an old-timey barbaric yawp spontaneously invented and then ritually reenacted.

Starting in the 1980s as well, rich Americans were given permission— by Reaganism, by the media, by themselves—to behave more like rich people in the old days, showing off their wealth. Conspicuous consumption had never disappeared, of course, but in the thriving decades that followed the Depression and the war, the big economic winners were really not supposed to flaunt their good fortune, and cultural norms were in place to enforce discretion. When I was growing up in Omaha in the 1960s and '70s, no one there thought it remarkable that our local multimillionaire Warren Buffett lived in a nice normal house on a small lot among other nice normal houses on small lots in a neighborhood that wasn't the fanciest in town. What seemed remarkable, rather, was the twenty-thousand-square-foot house that the founder of Godfather's Pizza built in 1983, by common reckoning the first true *mansion* to go up in Omaha since the 1920s. Those national quiet-wealth norms were crumbling when a Rolls-Royce Owners' Club newsletter morphed into a successful glossy national magazine for and about the wealthy called *The Robb Report* (1976), and they'd evaporated entirely when *Lifestyles of the Rich and Famous* went on the air (1984) to persuade people that the lives of the fictional superrich on *Dallas* (1978) and *Dynasty* (1981) were real—get a load of this *Glengarry*–meets–*Wall Street* Iacocca-Welch impersonator Donald Trump!—and that ostentatious personal wealth was now the only American Dream that mattered.

Our fantasy-industrial complex also reflected and normalized the new old-fashioned laissez-faire rules by making legal gambling ubiquitous, like in the Old West and in old Europe. Until the late 1980s, only two U.S. states allowed commercial casino gambling, but within a decade, legal casinos existed in half the states. Before the 1970s, only two state governments operated lotteries, but most did by the end of the 1980s, a decade states also spent cutting taxes. In addition to the bad odds of winning, the state-run numbers rackets really amount to a crypto-tax, maybe the most regressive ever, since lottery players are disproportionately poor.

I don't think it was coincidence that this happened simultaneously with the U.S. political economy metaphorically turning into a winner-take-all casino economy. The gambling hall replaced the factory floor as our governing economic symbol, a flashy, totally temporary gathering of magical-thinking individual strangers whose fortunes depend overwhelmingly on luck instead of on collective hard work with trusted industrious colleagues day after day. Risk-taking is a good thing, central to much of America's success, but not when the risks are involuntary for everyone except the people near the top, required rather than freely chosen, and when those at the top have arranged things so they don't have much serious downside risk. As Americans were herded into literal casinos, they were simultaneously being herded en masse into our new national economic casino, where the games were rigged in favor of the well-to-do players.

People put up with it, for the same reason that the great mass of people in casinos put up with playing games that the house always wins in the long run. The spectacle of a few ecstatic individual winners at that poker table or the screaming slot machine over there makes the losers envious but not resentful and encourages them to believe that, hey, they too might get lucky and win.

After all, for as long as anyone could remember, Americans shared *proportionately* in the national prosperity, the fractions going to the people at the bottom and the middle and the top all growing at the same rate. In the 1980s it wasn't yet clear to most people that the political economy was being changed from a more or less win-win game to one that was practically zero-sum, that over the next few decades, at least three-quarters of them would be the economic casino's suckers, that their losses and forgone winnings would all go to the luckiest 20 percent, and that thenceforth in America *only* the rich would get much richer.

That's because the successful and comfortable social contract that had been in effect in America from the 1930s was replaced by a new one. Social contracts are unwritten but real, taken seriously but not literally, which is their beauty and their problem. They consist of all the principles and norms governing how members of society are expected to treat one another, the balance between economic rights and responsibilities, between how much freedom is permitted and how much fairness is re-quired. All the formal rules specifying behavioral constraints and respon-sibilities, the statutes and bureaucratic codes, are distinct from the social contract but overlap with it, because lots of the specific rules—tax rates, minimum wages, environmental regulations, the cost of education—are codifications of the social contract.

Contracts are negotiated, ideally in a way that all the signatories feel fairly treated. In the evolving American social contract, the balance among the competing demands of liberty and equality and solidarity (or *fraternité*) worked pretty well for most of the twentieth century, the arc bending toward justice. But then came the ultra-individualistic frenzy of the 1960s, and during the 1970s and '80s, liberty assumed its powerfully politicized form and eclipsed equality and solidarity among our aspira-tional values. *Greed is good* meant that selfishness lost its stigma. And that was when we were in trouble.

The best test of a morally legitimate social contract is a thought ex-periment that the philosopher John Rawls named the Veil of Ignorance in 1971, just as modern American ultra-individualism exploded. The idea is to imagine you know nothing of your actual personal circumstances—wealth, abilities, education, race, ethnicity, gender, age; all those salient facts are *veiled* from you. Would you agree to sign your country's social contract and take your chances for better or worse in the social and politi-cal and economic system it governs?

Conservatives and the well-to-do in particular should submit to this test. A central tenet of economic libertarianism is the importance of lit-eral contracts: if people sign a contract freely agreeing to its terms, it's their business and nobody else's what they do for or to one another. But "*social* contracts"? Fuck you, you do-gooders and losers and moochers. Libertarians fantasize that they're action heroes and entirely self-made. They tend to exempt themselves from the truism that there but for the grace of God goes each one of them, because an implicit premise of their ultra-individualism is that anybody in America can make it on their own and that unfair disadvantages either don't exist or can't be helped. I have a hunch that the demographic profile of self-identified libertarians—94 percent white, 68 percent male, 62 percent in their forties or younger—has something to do with those beliefs and fantasies.

14

How Wall Street Ate America

The ugly, confusing word *financialization* was invented in the late 1960s, the period of Peak New, just before America entered the era of extreme financialization. But it didn't really become a common term until we all first experienced one of its spectacularly ugly, confusing, and destructive results, the market crash and meltdown of 2008.

Simply put, financialization is how Wall Street effectively took over the U.S. economy during the fourth quarter of the twentieth century. Our economy's main players and private stewards went from a focus on actual work and production of goods and services to a preoccupation with financial scheming around productive enterprises and the work they do.

It was another paradigm shift. Financialization happening in sync with the other plotlines and big shifts in this book was not a coincidence. The changes were all of a piece and synergistic. Wall Street's new hegemony was first enabled by Milton Friedman's mainstreamed libertarianism and then reinforced it in turn—ditto with financialization and deregulation, the Law and Economics movement, the atrophying of antitrust, the lionization of guys like Jack Welch and Gordon Gekko, the digital revolution, increasingly short-term thinking, only adjust, and share the pain of slower growth in their own globalizing, automating economies. In America, however, as a result of the new right-wing, favor-the-rich, big-business-rules charter, only the well-educated and well-to-do continued to get bigger pieces of our more slowly growing economic pie. And not only did the *size* of the pieces of pie served to the unlucky American majority stop getting bigger, the *quality* of those relatively skimpy pieces got worse: jobs and healthcare and retirements became more insecure, cities and regions were left to wither, college education became much less affordable, and upward mobility was a longer shot than ever.

I've relied on the metaphor of an American economic pie to convey how only the luckiest few kept getting served good, larger pieces as it grew. But that may be another metaphor that's too benign for how the economy changed starting in the 1970s and '80s. It's more like this: after surviving the Depression and winning the war, Americans cruised along together for almost four decades in glorious sunny weather that seemed like it would go on forever—then we hit rough seas, and suddenly the first-class passengers, saying they hoped everyone else could join them later, grabbed all the lifeboats for themselves and sped off to their own private luxury ship anchored in a safe harbor.

Joseph Schumpeter was a brilliant economist at Harvard in the first half of the twentieth century who approved of entrepreneurs but also thought capitalism would eventually be replaced by some kind of democratic socialism—not through workers' uprisings but by means of a subtle, non-violent process. The "perennial gale of *creative destruction*" would drive this evolution of advanced economic systems, he wrote (without italics) in 1942, right after the Depression, "the same process of industrial mutation—if I may use that biological term—that incessantly revolutionizes the economic structure from within, incessantly destroying the old one, incessantly creating a new one. This process of Creative Destruction is the essential fact about capitalism."

I feel sorry for Schumpeter, who died in 1950, because three decades after his death, with the rise of new-fangled old-fashioned free-market mania, he got famous when that phrase was revived and reduced to a meme, repeated endlessly to explain and justify the sudden obsolescence of blue-collar production workers (and then the lesser white-collar workers). "Creative destruction" was popularized in a way Schumpeter hadn't meant it, as a celebratory sorry-suckers catchphrase for the way rootin'-tootin' Wild West American capitalism permanently *is,* where the rich and tough and lucky win and losers lose hard. In the 1980s the term and its distorted meaning were enthusiastically embraced by the right and accepted with a shrug by college-educated liberals whose livelihoods didn't look likely to be creatively destroyed anytime soon by competition from computers or foreigners.

We liberals had heard of Schumpeter, and we knew a bit about the industrial revolutions at the turns of the previous two centuries. My professor in the 1970s, Daniel Bell, had predicted this difficult turn more than two decades earlier in a book called *Work and Its Discontents: The Cult of Efficiency in America.* Thanks to automation, he said, "many workers, particularly older ones, may find it difficult ever again to find suitable jobs. It is also likely that small geographical pockets of the United States may find themselves becoming 'depressed areas' as old industries fade or are moved away." We college-educateds were instructed to take it as a truism that painful transitions like these were just how history and economic progress inevitably unfolded, and that after a difficult patch—for the actual, you know, *workers,* in what we started calling the Rust Belt—things would eventually sort themselves out.

That long view, however, tended to omit the history that had made the previous industrial revolutions come out okay in America—the countervailing forces that took a century to build, all the laws and rules and unions and other organizations created to protect citizens and workers and keep the system reasonably fair and balanced. It was exactly that web of countervailing forces that, at exactly that moment, was being systematically weakened.

The fraction of all American workers employed in manufacturing peaked in the 1950s, but the actual *number* of those jobs had held steady through the 1960s and '70s. In 1980 manufacturing workers' salaries and benefits still provided the livings for a third of all Americans. But then came this latest wave of creative destruction, and that was that. The collapse of the steel industry came right around 1980—spectacularly, because most of us hadn't seen it coming, and steel plants were so gigantic, and geographically concentrated, each one the economic foundation of a town or city or whole region. Those were well-paid union jobs that had seemed secure. In and around Pittsburgh during the 1980s, unemployment rates at their lingering height—15 percent, 20 percent, 27 percent—were the same as the rates all over America during the Depression of the 1930s (and once again in 2020).

It wasn't just the steel industry that was undone, of course. Almost 3 million U.S. manufacturing jobs disappeared in just three years. In 1980 one of the huge textile company Parkdale Mills's plants in South Carolina employed 2,000 people—but by the 1990s, thanks to more efficient machinery, that factory was producing just as much fabric with only 140 employees, 93 percent fewer workers. That's an extreme case but a microcosm of what was starting to happen throughout manufacturing. By the end of the century, U.S. factories were producing two-thirds more things than they had in 1980, but they were doing so with a third fewer workers.

And when new machines couldn't do the work more cheaply than people, then people in poor countries could become our slavish machine equivalents as never before. Starting in the late 1980s and especially the 1990s, more and more of our manufacturing work was done in China and other poor countries. Between 1990 and the early 2000s, the annual value of things made in China and bought by Americans increased twelvefold. Many millions of U.S. factory jobs were "offshored" during the 1990s and early 2000s, many of them to China. From 1980 until now, the fraction of Americans working in factories shrank by two-thirds, from more than one in four workers to fewer than one in twelve.

The new jobs to which laid-off workers moved, during and after the 1980s, tended to be much worse than the ones they'd had. A massive study by economists of "high-tenure workers laid off then from distressed firms" in Pennsylvania—including steelworkers—found that years after they lost those jobs, their incomes remained much lower. For instance, the average Pennsylvania worker whose job disappeared in early 1982 had been earning the equivalent of $53,000 a year, but six years later he or she was earning only $34,000 in today's dollars. That $19,000-per-year reduction in average earnings was as if they'd all been involuntarily transported back in time to the 1940s, those three decades of accumulated American prosperity instantly erased.

As I explained earlier, for centuries new technologies had kept making it possible for each worker to produce more stuff, and it was that, improving productivity, that allowed economies to grow, and more people to live well. For the last century and a half, from the late 1800s on, productivity in America increased most years by 2 percent or more. There were ups and downs in the trend line, of course—dramatically down during the Great Depression, exceptionally up for some years right after World War II. Along the way, new technologies made some jobs uneconomic and unnecessary. But because of the grand economic bargain we had in America to bring everyone along through those ups and downs and changes, to share the increasing wealth, *everyone's* standard of living increased over time, slower some years, faster other years, but always in sync. During the three postwar decades, U.S. productivity doubled, and the size of the U.S. economy doubled, and the average American's share of the economy doubled. Then, from the late 1970s through the '80s, we experienced a subpar slough, a fifteen-year period when productivity increased by just 1 to 2 percent a year instead of 2 to 3 percent.*

As so many switches flipped, nobody would see the full effects until decades later. The productivity of workers and economic growth both continued going up, albeit more slowly, almost doubling since the 1970s. But for the first time, *most Americans' incomes* essentially flatlined for forty years. Instead of everyone, rich and middle and poor, all becoming more prosperous simultaneously, only the incomes of a lucky top fifth kept rising as they had in the past. Around 1980, the Great Uncoupling of the rich from the rest began.

It wasn't just that serious salary increases started going only to a small group of fortunate workers. The share of money that went to *all employees,* rather than to corporate shareholders and business owners, also became smaller. Until 1980, America's national split of "gross domestic income" was around 60–40 in favor of workers, but then it began dropping and is now approaching 50–50. That change amounts to almost $1 trillion a year, an annual average of around $5,000 that each person with a job *isn't* being paid. Instead, every household in the top 1 percent of earners has been getting $700,000 extra every year. It undoubtedly has been the largest and fastest upward redistribution of wealth in history.

---

*We entered a similar productivity slough after the Great Recession, which seemed to be ending just before the 2020 recession.

This historic Great Uncoupling, in which America's economy grows but most Americans don't get fair shares of the growth, was the result of the public and private policy choices described in this book and hundreds more. I don't think most of the people who engineered and benefited from the remaking of the political economy consciously intended for most of their fellow citizens' incomes to stagnate forever. Driven variously by ideology and selfishness, big business and the rich wanted more wealth and power for themselves, but surely most wouldn't have *objected* if everyone's boats had kept rising together after 1980, if the middle-of-the-pack family earning $50,000 then was now earning $100,000 instead of $55,000.

But there's the disingenuous rub. It's as if I'd abandoned my wife and children and thereafter gave them as little money as I could get away with legally, but said sincerely that I hadn't *intended* to make their lives so difficult but, you know, *sorry*. Because the major drivers of America's economic transformation after 1980—from low taxes to the laissez-faire unleashing of business to reflexive opposition to new social programs to the crushing of organized labor—guaranteed the massively unfair outcome. And while perhaps the CEOs at the Business Roundtable in the 1970s didn't explicitly say their mission was to make their employees much more insecure and thus more compliant and cowering—by laying off thousands at a time, phasing out pensions, moving factories overseas, and eliminating competitors—that's what happened.

The shocking cataclysm in America's big, iconic heavy industries, steel and cars, along with the longer-term slowing of economic growth generally, created a chronic widespread dread and anxiety about the economic future. The economic right and big business *used* that confusion and fear to get free rein to achieve their larger goals. *Times are tough! Government can't save you! Adapt or die!* But then when the acute crises passed and the economy stabilized in the late 1980s and '90s, and productivity and economic growth returned to their long-term historical norms, the norms of *fairness* were *not* restored. The system that had been reengineered to better serve big business and the rich remained in place.

Because I'm an American who graduated college and as an adult haven't been paid to do physical labor, I've never thought of myself as a *worker*.

It's too bad, I think, because since the 1960s that linguistic distinction has reinforced the divide between people who do white-collar and blue-collar work. We're nearly all workers, rather than people who live off investments. Looking back now, probably the single most significant cause *and* effect of the big 1980s change in our political economy was the disempowerment of workers vis-à-vis employers.

A few years ago when I first read the book *Postcapitalism* by the British business journalist Paul Mason, I came across a paragraph that stopped me short because it seemed so hyperbolic and reductive. But now it seems to me very much closer to true than untrue. In the 1970s and '80s, Mason says, the political leaders from the economic right

> drew a conclusion that has shaped our age: that a modern economy cannot coexist with an organized working class. . . . The destruction of labour's bargaining power . . . was the essence of the entire [conservative] project: it was a means to all the other ends . . . not free markets, not fiscal discipline, not sound money, not privatization and offshoring—not even globalization. All these things were byproducts or weapons of its main endeavor: to remove organized labor from the equation.

As the modern corporation emerged and grew and multiplied starting in the late 1800s, so did unions. In the 1880s fewer than 5 percent of American workers belonged to a union, and in 1930 it was still only around 10 percent. But after the Depression and New Deal and World War II, more than a third of the U.S. private workforce was unionized, and in 1950 a large majority of blue-collar workers in the North belonged to unions. In the late 1950s state laws started changing so that teachers and other public employees could also join unions, and eventually more than a third of them became unionized. As labor unions grew larger and more powerful, negotiating higher salaries, America's wealth was more and more equally shared.

As I've said, by the 1960s and '70s, Americans were taking for granted the benefits and prosperity that organized labor had been crucial in achieving for workers in general, and many were becoming disenchanted with unions. After the unionization of workers at corporations peaked in the 1950s, that overall percentage slid to a quarter by the early 1970s—just when big business and the right started powerfully organizing capital to *really* fight against organized labor.

In 1979 moviegoers, especially liberal moviegoers, made a hit out of the movie *Norma Rae*. Sally Field won an Academy Award for playing the title role. It was based on the true story of a J. P. Stevens textile factory worker in North Carolina who organized a union and a successful strike—which led quickly to the unionization of three thousand textile workers at other plants in the same town. The real events had happened only a few years earlier, so the movie encouraged viewers to imagine, incorrectly, that U.S. labor power wasn't half-dead—yet it simultaneously played as wistful nostalgia.

The political winds had definitely shifted. Also in 1979 public TV producers at WGBH in Boston were developing a ten-episode dramatic series called *Made in USA* about the history of the labor movement. They'd planned on having unions put up a quarter of the budget—but in early 1980, the president of PBS in Washington stepped in to forbid that, because unions had a political agenda. After it was pointed out that Milton Friedman's PBS series *Free to Choose*, airing right then (including the antiunion episode "Who Protects the Worker?"), was funded by corporations and rich people with a political agenda, PBS relented, but after the controversy and then Reagan's election in the fall, that project died.

Consider what happened to political action committees, the tremendous new sources of campaign donations. From 1976 on, another two or three business-funded PACs were created *every week* on average, compared to one union-funded PAC every few months. In the early 1970s, union PACs were still donating *most* of the PAC money going to U.S. Senate and House candidates; by 1980 they were donating not just much less than the business groups but less than a quarter of the total given by all PACs.

In 1977 President Carter declined to work hard for a bill that would've given construction workers greater power to strike, and it was defeated in the House, where Democrats had a two-to-one majority. The next year the same Congress was considering a labor law change that would've made it easier for all workers to unionize. The CEOs of fully unionized GM and GE were disinclined to oppose the bill, but their fellow Business Roundtable member who ran the barely unionized Sears persuaded them to lobby against it—and capitalist solidarity carried the day. It too was defeated. Carter and most Democrats shrugged.

That was a final straw for the president of the United Automobile Workers (and Lee Iacocca's good pal), Douglas Fraser. At the time, the White House regularly convened a semiofficial Labor-Management Group that brought together CEOs, many of them members of the new Roundtable, with union leaders. "I know that some of the business representatives . . . argued inside the Business Roundtable for neutrality" on the bill, Fraser wrote in his letter resigning from the White House group in 1978, "but having lost, they helped to bankroll (through the Roundtable and other organizations) the dishonest and ugly multimillion-dollar [publicity and lobbying] campaign against labor law reform" that "stands as the most vicious, unfair attack upon the labor movement in more than 30 years. Corporate leaders knew it was not the 'power grab by Big Labor' that they portrayed it to be." He went on to deliver an impassioned realtime critique of the axiomatic shift just beginning:

> The leaders of industry, commerce and finance in the United States have broken and discarded the fragile, unwritten compact previously existing during a past period of growth and progress. . . . At virtually every level, I discern a demand by business for docile government and unrestrained corporate individualism. Where industry once yearned for subservient unions, it now wants no unions at all.

If destroying labor's bargaining power was the essence of the project of the economic right, its essential act was performed single-handedly by Ronald Reagan six months into his presidency.

The typical air traffic controller was an archetypal Reagan Democrat—a white man from a working-class background without a college degree but highly skilled and well paid. In the late 1960s, the controllers in New York had started a union, the Professional Air Traffic Controllers Organization (PATCO), which before long almost all controllers in the United States joined. Two weeks before the 1980 election, it was one of the very few unions to endorse Reagan against the preachy, unreliable Democrat in the White House. "You supports them that supports you," one of the top PATCO leaders explained, "and you don't support them that don't support you." That is, when you can't count on Democrats *or* Republicans to support you on your economic issues, you might as well support the ones who agree with you about hippies and professors and welfare recipients.

Two weeks after Reagan became president, his administration began negotiating a new contract with the controllers, who were federal employees. The ultimate leverage any union has, obviously, is the threat that its members will stop working if they and their employers can't come to terms. The same bit of the U.S. criminal code that prohibits any federal employee from advocating the overthrow of the government, enacted in 1955 during the anti-Communist frenzy, also makes it a crime for any of them to go out on strike. A couple of times a year during the 1960s and '70s, groups of federal employees had stopped working to get what they wanted, including a weeklong wildcat strike by a minority of postal workers in 1970, but no federal workers had ever officially threatened to cut off essential services to get a better labor contract. Push had never really come to shove.

PATCO was thus in a singularly powerful and precarious position. No civilian federal employees had more strike-threat leverage than air traffic controllers: all of U.S. aviation and thus the U.S. economy depended on them. Right before their contract expired in the spring of 1981, the brand-new president had survived his assassination attempt, which increased Americans' approval of him to 68 percent. The controllers were already earning the equivalent of $100,000 a year on average and now asked for a 40 percent increase in pay, a four-day work week, and retirement after twenty years. Union leaders agreed to a lesser deal, but then the members rejected it.

Liberals were not in solidarity with PATCO. A *New York Times* editorial headlined BRING THE CONTROLLERS DOWN TO EARTH said that "the Reagan Administration is making a more than reasonable offer" in response to "the union's exorbitant terms," and a later editorial said that if "President Reagan were now to sweeten the deal . . . he would only be inviting other Government employees in key positions to exploit their leverage." In *The Washington Monthly*, twenty-three-year-old Jonathan

Alter, just out of Harvard and not yet a celebrated liberal journalist and author, wrote that the episode "proved" Reagan and the right correct, that the federal government was bloated, "as badly featherbedded as we've feared."

The lead-up to the strike was a big national story for months, then the biggest for some weeks. First thing in the morning on the first Monday in August 1981, when the *Times* ran another anti-PATCO editorial (HOLDING UP AMERICA), the thirteen thousand controllers stopped working. Reagan said they had two days to come back, and on Wednesday the 90 percent who didn't were fired—and prohibited from holding any federal job ever again.* Two months later the fired strikers' replacements took a vote to get rid of the union, and that was that.

The strike-day *Times* editorial said that it was "hard to feel much sympathy for the controllers." Sure. In retrospect, however, it's hard not to feel some sympathy for them, and even more, it's hard not to feel deep regret that so many left-of-center Americans had abandoned the fundamental commitment to the *idea* of unions. The air traffic controllers' strike and the right-wing president's instant, unchallenged destruction of their union was the turning point. Losing that battle, American organized labor effectively lost the war.

As part of the New Deal, a fundamental federal law had been passed guaranteeing employees of businesses the right to organize unions and go on strike. Three years later, in 1938, the Supreme Court ruled that the Mackay Radio & Telegraph Company had broken that law after a strike by refusing specifically to rehire its organizers—but the court's decision also said, in passing, that not only were companies free to hire replacement workers during strikes but that after a strike ended, companies were free to keep employing the strikebreakers. The strikers' only right was to be rehired for any additional jobs that might open up soon. The logic of that Mackay Doctrine, that strikers aren't technically *fired* if they're replaced by scabs, is absurd. Despite that 1938 decision, the American *norm* that emerged out of the New Deal was that for companies to replace striking workers was unacceptably unfair—a norm that remained in force until its spectacular de facto repeal by Reagan during the air traffic controllers' strike.

---

*After a dozen years, the Clinton administration lifted that ban on federal employment.

In the years right after the 1981 strike, companies all over the country made and remade the point again and again—big strike, strikebreakers brought in, national press attention, strike continued and disastrously failed, unions dissolved or rendered impotent. And the old Mackay Doctrine, which had sat on a back shelf for half a century, let them.

One of the big American mining companies realized that the moment for good-old-days antiunion ferocity had returned: a year after a strike began in Arizona and the company replaced striking copper miners with strikebreakers, its workers all over the Southwest were persuaded to do away with their unions.

A year after that the meat company Hormel demanded that its slaughterhouse workers take a one-quarter cut in wages that hadn't gone up in almost a decade. Workers at a Minnesota plant went on strike, strikebreakers were hired, and most of the strikers never got their jobs back.

International Paper had tripled its profits from 1985 to 1987—but as a recently public company, its 10 percent rate of profit wasn't good enough anymore to satisfy the demands of shareholder supremacy, so its executives decided to end the company's long history of worker-friendliness. In a town in Maine where the International Paper mill was everything, and typical workers earned the equivalent of $87,000 a year, the union made an opening bid to renew their contract with no wage increase at all. The company responded with a plan to lay off 15 percent of them and, for those remaining, do away with extra pay on weekends and holidays. The workers went on strike, the company hired replacements from out of town, a year later the strikers surrendered, and sorry, no job openings, bye.

Hiring strikebreakers, for decades a rarity in corporate America because it had been considered old-fashioned and brutish, was *back*, old-fashioned and tough: during the late 1980s, more than a third of the companies where workers went on strike threatened to replace the strikers, and half of those did.

The deterrent effect was extreme. Strikes very quickly became almost obsolete, like vinyl LPs and rotary-dial telephones. Between World War II and 1980, our great era of prosperity and increasing equality, almost every year there had been at least two hundred strikes involving at least a thousand workers. Some years there were more than four hundred big strikes. Since 1981, there haven't been a hundred big strikes in any year, and in this century there have never been more than twenty-two in a year. As recently as the early 1970s, 2.5 million American workers would go on strike in a given year, but 1979 was the last time that more than a million went out. It doesn't seem like coincidence that the rise and fall of strikes during the twentieth century correlates very closely with the rise and sudden stagnation of U.S. wages.

After the don't-make-scabs-permanent norm was abandoned in the 1980s, Democrats tried to get their act together, kind of, early in the next decade. The House passed a bill to outlaw what was now happening—companies effectively firing strikers for striking. Remember how back in the 1970s *The Washington Post* had hired permanent replacements for its striking pressmen, thus busting that union? Twenty years later, when the bill prohibiting that got to the Senate, the *Post* editorialized against it as "a sop to organized labor" and "bad legislation"—because sometimes "strikers by their behavior forfeit the right of return and companies ought to hire permanent replacements. This newspaper faced such a breach in dealing with one of its unions in the 1970s." Days later, despite a large Democratic majority in the Senate, the prospective law was filibustered to death by the Republican minority.

Labor law isn't only a federal matter. During the New Deal, unions began signing contracts with company managements that required workers to join their unions or at least to pay union dues so there would be no free riders. Soon businesses and the political right started lobbying state legislatures to outlaw such contracts, shrewdly calling the proposed statutes "right-to-work" laws. And then in 1947, during one of just four years between 1933 and 1995 when Republicans controlled both the House and the Senate, Congress amended the National Labor Relations Act to give states permission to enact such antiunion laws. By 1955, seventeen states had done so, mostly in the South. But then the right-to-work movement stalled, and for almost a quarter-century it seemed dead—until the late 1970s and '80s. Today most states have right-to-work laws, all but two of them states that voted Republican in the 2016 presidential election.

Studying America's organized labor history, I noticed a symmetry that seems to show a tipping point: the moment when the fraction of all workers belonging to unions hits 25 percent. During the New Deal, that fraction zoomed from less than 10 percent past 25 percent in a decade. It was still 25 percent in the mid-1970s, but then as the right's Raw Deal forced what had gone up to keep coming down, the percentage plummeted to 10 percent by the 1990s for workers in the private sector, and it kept on shrinking, down to 6 percent today—a level of unionization back to what it was in the very early 1900s. *Most* of the decline in unionization during the last half-century happened just during the 1980s.* Once again, it's remarkable how much the American 1980s amounted to the 1930s in reverse.

Employers in the '80s also started using as never before a clever, quieter way of paying low-wage workers even less and neutering their unions: contracting with private firms to do blue-collar service work. This technique proved especially popular among public and nonprofit entities like colleges and cities, for whom the optics and politics of directly nickel-and-diming laborers and security guards could be awkward.

Harvard, for instance, employed a couple of thousand people as guards, janitors, parking attendants, and cooks, most of them unionized. Then in the 1980s and '90s, the university started outsourcing much of that work to private contractors—contractors that paid lower wages and used nonunion workers. After that the threat of outsourcing still more jobs loomed over all of Harvard's negotiations with its own unionized workers, which persuaded them to accept lower wages: between 1980 and 1996, their pay actually *fell* from the equivalent of $600 or $700 a week to $500 or $600.† Or consider the people paid to schlep baggage onto and off of planes at U.S. airports. In 2002, 75 percent of them were employed directly by airlines; by 2012, 84 percent of them worked for outside contractors, and their average hourly wage had been cut almost in half, to less than twelve dollars.

Until I started researching this book, I'd never thought about this new wrinkle in the economy, let alone understood its scale or impact. Like so many of the hundreds of changes instituted in the 1980s, the practice of replacing staff with contract workers was too arcane and te-

---

*Because the unionization of *government* workers only happened in the 1960s and '70s, just before the right started its full-bore campaign to turn back time and diminish workers' power, more than a third of public-sector employees were in unions by 1980, and they still are.

†Because it was Harvard, protests and ambient liberalism and an endowment of $18 billion in 2002 persuaded its president—Larry Summers, who'd just served as Clinton's secretary of the treasury—to start paying those service workers good wages after a generation of stiffing them.

dious for many of the rest of us to care or even know about. But imagine the thousands of companies and cities and schools and cultural institutions all over the country that have delegated so much of this kind of work to contractors, thereby making the treatment of all those eleven-dollar-an-hour workers somebody else's problem. According to a 2018 study by five major-university economists, a full *third* of the increase in American income inequality over these last forty years has been the result of just this one new, dehumanizing labor practice.

Another cunning way big businesses began squeezing workers in the 1980s was to become *extremely* big. "The basic idea," explains an economist specializing in markets for labor, "is that if employers don't have to compete with one another for workers, they can pay less, and workers will be stuck without the outside job offers that would enable them to claim higher wages."

As antitrust enforcement was discredited and enfeebled starting in the 1970s, big corporations were able to get so big and dominant in their business or regions that they had ever fewer companies directly competing with them to hire workers. More and more of them became the only games in town. One of the scholars who has helped expose this particular bit of rigging and its unfairness over the last several decades is the influential, idiosyncratic University of Chicago law professor Eric Posner.* As he and his economist co-author Glen Weyl explain, antitrust laws were enacted to make sure that businesses compete in every way—not just as *sellers* setting the prices they charge for products and services, but also as *buyers* of labor setting the salaries they pay. The appeal of antitrust for citizens was to make sure competition kept prices lower and salaries higher. Enforcement of our antitrust laws, however, has come to focus entirely on consumer prices, particularly since the definitive Borking of the field in the late 1970s. The antitrust enforcers at the Department of Justice and Federal Trade Commission, because they rely "on the traditional assumption that labor markets are competitive," and that it wasn't *their* jobs to protect workers anyhow, "have never blocked a merger because of its effect on labor," and they don't even employ experts who

---

*He's the son of the influential, idiosyncratically conservative University of Chicago law professor, antitrust expert, and former federal judge Richard Posner, who helped transform antitrust and other economic law to help business.

could calculate those effects. If two rival companies made a secret agreement to cap workers' salaries, they could get sued, but since "mergers that dramatically increase [companies'] labor market power are allowed with little objection," the companies can combine and thereby create a salary-squeezing employment monopoly.*

Companies don't even need to merge in order to pay workers less than they'd have to pay in a truly free labor market. I'd assumed only high-end employees were ever required to sign noncompete contracts—an HBO executive prohibited from going to work at Netflix, a coder at Lyft who can't take a job coding for Uber. But no: shockingly, noncompetes have come to be used just as much to prevent a $10-an-hour fry cook at Los Pollos Hermanos from quitting to work for $10.75 at Popeyes. Of all American workers making less than $40,000 a year, one in eight are bound by noncompete agreements. As another way to reduce workers' leverage, three-quarters of fast-food franchise chains have contractually prohibited their restaurant operators from hiring workers away from fellow franchisees.

Starting in the 1980s, the federal government also instituted big, covert structural tilts in favor of business—examples of the sneaky, stealthy "drift" effect I mentioned earlier. Inflation was an important tool for the economic right to get its way—first politically in 1980, when rapidly rising prices helped them get power, and thereafter by letting normal inflation move money from employees to employers by means of a kind of macroeconomic magician's trick. Instead of actually *repealing* two important New Deal laws that had helped workers for four decades, an essentially invisible ad hoc regime of gradual, automatic pay cuts was put in place. One involved overtime pay, time and a half for each hour an employee works over forty a week—which legally goes only to people with salaries below a certain level. The new ploy was to stop raising that salary threshold in the late 1970s, or the '80s, or the '90s—thus letting inflation constantly lower it, thereby continually reducing the number of people who qualified for overtime pay. In 1975, when the threshold was the equivalent of $56,000 a year, a large majority of U.S. workers were eligible; in 2019, after just a single increase since 1975, the overtime line

---

*Economists' term for markets where there's just one overwhelmingly dominant buyer of labor (or anything else) is a *monopsony*.

was under $24,000, which meant that fewer than 7 percent of American workers qualified.

A similar surreptitious screwing-by-inaction is how the federal minimum wage was dramatically reduced over time. From the mid-1950s until 1980, the minimum wage had been the equivalent of $10 or $12 an hour in today's dollars. As with overtime pay, the minimum wage was never technically *reduced*, but by 1989 inflation had actually reduced it to just over $7, where it remains today. In other words, it has been the federal government's unspoken decision to cut the wages of America's lowest-paid workers by more than a third, a choice first made during the 1980s when it stopped raising the minimum, then ratified again and again by Democratic as well as Republican Congresses. In addition to keeping costs low for the employers of Kroger cashiers and Burger King cooks and Holiday Inn maids, the lower national floor for pay has the invisible-hand effect of pulling down the low wages of people earning more than the legal minimum.

Economic right-wingers have publicly *reveled* in their squashing of workers' power in so many different ways. Federal Reserve chair Alan Greenspan said in a speech in the 2000s that spectacularly firing and replacing all the striking air traffic controllers in 1981 had been "perhaps the most important domestic" accomplishment of the Reagan presidency.

> [It] gave weight to the legal right of *private* employers, previously not fully exercised, to use their own discretion to both hire and discharge workers. There was great consternation among those who feared that an increased ability to lay off workers would amplify the sense of job insecurity. Whether the average level of job insecurity has risen is difficult to judge.

In fact, it began a cascading increase in job insecurity throughout the U.S. economy that wasn't at all difficult to see and feel and measure.

16

Insecurity Is a Feature, Not a Bug

W hen I was a little kid, whenever we had to play musical chairs in school or at birthday parties, I never enjoyed it. I hated the tense seconds of waiting for each drop of the needle onto the record. Musical chairs made me anxious and made everyone manic and delivered a nasty set of lessons—life is an accelerating competition of one against all for diminishing resources, survival is just a matter of luck and a touch of brute force, and success is a momentary feeling of superiority to the losers who lose before you lose, with just one out of the ten or twenty of us a winner.

Working on this book, I've thought again and again of that game, how the rules of our economy were rewritten as a high-stakes game of musical chairs, with more anxiety and dread and frenzy. In fact, our economy since 1980 has been a particularly sadistic version of the game, where some players are disabled or don't know the rules, and in addition to winning, only the winners get cake and ice cream and rides home.

The crippling of organized labor since 1980—and the increase in automation and relocating work abroad—helped make most American workers more anxious and uncertain and less prosperous. But there are other ways that increasing insecurity and increasing inequality got built into the political economy and became features of the system more than bugs.

The Friedman Doctrine in 1970 begat the shareholder supremacy movement in the 1980s, which begat an unraveling of all the old norms concerning loyalty and decency of businesses toward employees. *Loyalty* implies treating employees better than the law requires, which was at odds with the new mandates of shareholder supremacy. Replacing strikers was a shock-and-awe swerve, outsourcing work to low-wage contractors a less dramatic form of cold-bloodedness. Both were highly effective means of scaring workers in order to reduce their power and keep their pay lower.

But once the norms changed and a higher stock price became every public company's practically exclusive goal, companies that weren't facing strikes or financial problems also embraced the new ruthlessness. In addition to GE and its rank-and-yank corporate copycats continually, automatically firing a fixed quota of employees, profitable corporations began firing workers in bulk simply to please the finance professionals who constitute the stock market. "In the 1980s," says Adam Cobb, a University of Pennsylvania Wharton School business professor who studies this sudden change in norms, "you started to see healthy firms laying off workers, mainly for shareholder value." IBM, for instance, abandoned its proud de facto promise of permanent employment—starting in 1990, it got rid of 41 percent of its workers in five years, at first softly, pensioning off people fifty-five and over, then after that using straight mass firings. Throughout U.S. corporate culture, it was as if a decent civilization abruptly reverted to primitivism, the powers-that-be in suits and ties propitiating the gods with human sacrifice—which in addition to increasing profits had the benefit of making the survivors cower before the ruling elite.

Other corporate norms that prevailed from the New Deal until the 1980s, in particular those providing *nonunion* employees with fixed-benefit pensions and good healthcare, had been enforced indirectly by the power of organized labor. Because "companies were very worried about unions and the possibility of strikes," another Wharton expert on labor relations explains, "they treated their employees well so they wouldn't join a union. But that is no longer the case. Unions are on the decline. It's easy to quash them if they try to organize. So some managers might not care as much about employee loyalty as they used to."

Jacob Hacker, the Yale political scientist, calls this the Great Risk Shift, the ways that starting around 1980, business, in order to reduce current and future costs, dumped more and more risk "back onto workers and their families." As a result, "problems once confined to the working poor—lack of health insurance and access to guaranteed pensions, job insecurity and staggering personal debt, bankruptcy and home foreclosure—have crept up the income ladder to become an increasingly normal part of middle-class life."

Health insurance became a standard part of American jobs starting in the 1940s and '50s, and early on the pioneering, not-for-profit, cover-everyone Blue Cross and Blue Shield associations provided most of that coverage. As commercial insurance companies got into the game, having Blue Cross and Blue Shield as their public interest competitors helped keep the for-profit insurers honest, not unlike how the existence of strong unions tended to make businesses treat nonunion employees better. In 1980 the three-quarters of Americans who had job-based health coverage paid very little in premiums or deductibles or copayments. But it's been all downhill from there, thanks to more mercilessly profit-obsessed employers and insurance companies and healthcare providers. More and more of the healthcare industry consisted of for-profit corporations that were more and more subject to stock price monomania. Since the 1990s in many states, Blue Cross and Blue Shield have become totally commercial for-profit insurance companies that (deceptively) continue to use the venerable nonprofit brand name. Moreover, barely half of Americans these days are covered by insurance provided by a breadwinner's employer. The average amount each American paid for medical expenses out of pocket increased by half during the 1980s alone. In 1980 the average family of four spent the equivalent of about $2,700 a year on medical expenses; today an average family of four—$50,000 income, insurance through the job—spends about $7,500 a year out of pocket.

The other existentially important benefit that American businesses began routinely offering in the 1950s was a fixed pension, a guaranteed monthly income for as long as you lived after you stopped working, which would be paid in addition to Social Security. Companies funded the pensions, and they became standard, like cover-almost-everything company-provided health insurance.

But then came the 1980s. I mentioned earlier how the tax code tweak 401(k), which went into effect in 1980, handed a captive audience of millions of new customers and a revenue bonanza to the financial industry.

But this innovation also provided a cost-cutting financial bonanza to employers. They now had another clever way to execute on the new Scrooge spirit: replacing the pensions they'd funded for decades with individual-worker-funded investment plans—self-reliance! freedom!—cost them less right away and cost them *nothing* once employee number 49732 left the building for good.

In a recent study, Adam Cobb of the Wharton School found that just as CEOs started satisfying their new Wall Street über-headquarters and shareholder supremacy dogma by laying off workers, they started getting rid of pensions for the same reason. At thirteen hundred of the biggest U.S. corporations from 1982 on, the more a company's shares were held by big financial institutions like mutual funds and banks—arm's-length overlords who definitely felt no loyalty to any particular company's employees—the more likely that company was to get rid of pension plans that had guaranteed benefits. On the other hand, companies that employed *any* unionized workers were likelier to continue paying pensions to their nonunion workers as well.

"The great lie is that the 401(k) was capable of replacing the old system of pensions," says the regretful man who was president of the American Society of Pension Actuaries at the time and who had given his strong endorsement to 401(k)s. Without any national conversation or meaningful protest by employees—without a union or a Congress that was prepared to step in, how did you push back?—this crucial clause in the modern American social contract was unilaterally eliminated. In 1980 eight out of ten large and medium-size companies paid a guaranteed monthly sum to retirees for life, and *most* American workers retired with a fixed pension on top of Social Security, which the pension often equaled. Today only one in eight private sector employees are in line to get such a pension, and most American workers don't even have a 401(k) or an IRA or any other retirement account. It's yet another route by which the U.S. political economy made a round trip from 1940 to 1980 and then back again.

I mentioned the libertarian Fed chair Alan Greenspan's remark that it was "difficult to judge" if the "increased ability to lay off workers" starting in the 1980s had had structurally, permanently increased Americans' "sense of job insecurity."

I am frequently concerned about being laid off. From 1979 through the 2000s, that statement was posed in a regular survey of employees of four hundred big U.S. corporations, each person asked if they agreed or disagreed. In 1982, early in our new national musical chairs game, during a bad recession with high unemployment, only 14 percent of this large sample of workers said they felt anxious about losing their jobs. The number crept upward during the 1980s, and then in the '90s people finally registered that, uh-oh, our social contract had been completely revamped. By 1995, even though the economic moment looked rosy— strong growth, the stock market rocketing upward—nearly half of Americans employed by big business said they worried a lot about being laid off.

In fact, in 1997, a strange new condition kicked in—pay continued to stagnate for most Americans despite low and dropping unemployment rates. A fundamental principle of free markets was being repudiated: the *supply* of labor could barely keep up with demand, but the *price* of labor, wages, wasn't increasing. Alan Greenspan, as he presented his semiannual economic report to the Senate Banking Committee, mentioned those survey results and testified that the surprising "softness in compensation growth" was "mainly the consequence of greater worker insecurity" that had arisen since the early 1980s, insecurity that was also responsible, he said, for the continuing "low level of work stoppages" by unionized workers.

In other words, employees of the biggest corporations, whose jobs everyone had considered the most secure, were now too frightened of being jettisoned from those jobs to push hard for more pay or better working conditions.

Those data and their implications must've slipped Greenspan's mind later when he found it "difficult to judge" the effects of insecurity on workers' leverage and pay. And he never mentioned, of course, that it was he and his confederates on the right who'd spent the last decades restructuring our political economy to reduce the power of workers and increase their job insecurity. He did say he thought the curious disconnect in the late 1990s—low unemployment but no pay increases—was a blip, that "the return to more normal patterns may be in process" already. But two decades later it remained the not-so-new normal. The long-standing balance of power between employers and the employed was completely changed.

The impact of suddenly higher insecurity was a cascade of more insecurity. Starting in the late 1980s, as soon as Greenspan's beloved new "ability to lay off workers" took effect, the fraction of Americans who actually lost their jobs each year increased by a third and stayed there. At the same time, individual household incomes started roller-coastering down and up and down as they hadn't before. Soon the household incomes of one in eight Americans, poor and affluent and in between, were dropping by half or more in any given two-year period. Between 1979 and 1991, personal bankruptcies tripled (and then doubled), and the mortgage foreclosure rate quadrupled (and then doubled).

At the same time that economic insecurity grew, new sources of economic inequality were built into our system that made insecurity more chronic and extreme. Scores of public and private choices and changes increased inequality, all shaped by the new governing economic gospel: everybody for themselves, everything's for sale, greed is good, the rich get richer, buyer beware, unfairness can't be helped, nothing but thoughts and prayers for the losers.

What happened with higher education is a prime example. College had been the great American portal to upward economic and social mobility, especially public universities, which give out two-thirds of all four-year undergraduate degrees. But in the 1980s, that portal started becoming much harder to get through financially *and* much more financially vital. Meanwhile the rapidly rising cost of college provided a new business opportunity for the ravenous financial industry, which beset graduates (and people who failed to graduate) with debt that made the chronic new economic insecurity even worse. If omnipotent sadists had set out to take an extremely good, well-functioning piece of our political economy and social structure and make it undemocratic and oppressive, this is what their scheme would've looked like.

When I graduated high school in the 1970s, I could've gone with a plurality of my friends to the University of Nebraska, for which my parents would've paid resident tuition, room, and board equivalent to $10,000 a year. But I got into Harvard, so I went there, which cost the equivalent of $22,000 a year, all in. Those prices were typical at the time. They were also the same as they'd been for public and high-end private colleges a decade earlier.

But then around 1980, under the camouflage of high inflation, private colleges started increasing their prices every year a bit *faster* than inflation. Public colleges soon followed suit, state legislatures started cutting university funding, and that vicious cycle picked up speed. In the 1990s the price of a college education ballooned even faster—especially at public institutions—and never stopped.

Since 1981 states have cut their funding of public colleges and universities by half. The real, inflation-adjusted cost of attending a four-year college has almost tripled. That undergraduate year at the University of Nebraska has gone from the equivalent of $10,000 in the 1970s to $25,000 now. The $22,000 that Harvard charged in the 1970s, which my parents could *just* scratch together, now runs $72,000 a year, all in.

Only a quarter of people graduating from four-year public colleges and universities in the early 1990s had student loan debt; by 2010, two-thirds did. Credit had been deregulated in the 1980s just in time for the business of student loans to explode in the '90s. When I graduated college in 1976, the total amount of money lent to students to pay for higher education each year was the equivalent of $8 billion—but by the first school year of the 1980s, it had jumped to $22 billion, and in 2005 it reached $100 billion. In other words, over those three decades, while the number of students grew by half, the amount of money they borrowed each year increased twelvefold. For the financial industry, a small revenue stream turned into a great roaring river. For the 45 million mostly young and youngish Americans who today carry an average of $35,000 apiece in student debt, it's yet another source of economic insecurity that did not exist before everything changed in the 1980s.

From the decade my parents attended college through the decade I attended college, the percentage of all Americans with four-year degrees more than tripled. But then college became terribly expensive, and that constant, rapid increase in people attending and graduating, hard evidence of the American Dream working, slowed *way* down, especially for men.

I'm fairly sure that an American college education today isn't two or three times as good as it was when I went, even though it's two or three times as expensive. Rather, in the 1980s *everything* in America became more of a commodity valued only by its market price, and a college degree was turned into a kind of luxury good, the way it had been back in my grandparents' day. But it wasn't just status anxiety that drove up the price of college in the 1980s, the decade in which Hermès started selling a certain leather handbag for ten thousand dollars apiece just because it could. A four-year degree simultaneously became an expensive luxury good *and* practically essential to a middle-class life, because the economic value of a degree also wildly increased during the 1980s and '90s.

College graduates had always been paid more on average than people with less education. But that college premium had actually *shrunk* during the twentieth century before 1950, and even after that didn't grow much—until 1980, when it exploded. In the early 1980s college graduates of all ages earned a third more than people who'd only graduated high school. Just a decade later, in 1992, they earned two-thirds more, as they still do. What's worse, for people who don't have college degrees, average real pay has gone *down* since then by 10 or 20 percent. In other words, a college degree became a more essential but also much less affordable ticket to the increasing prosperity that, until 1980, all Americans had enjoyed.

Yet in this century, there's a bait-and-switch lose-lose-lose punchline to the story. Since 2000, with two generations of college graduates having burdened themselves with unprecedented debt to pay for the unprecedented new costs of college, the college-grad income premium basically stopped increasing. Today four out of ten recent American college graduates are employed in jobs that don't even require a college degree. And while college graduates used to accumulate more wealth at younger ages than people without degrees, according to a 2018 Federal Reserve study, the costs of college and of student debt have now erased that wealth premium for younger college-educated Americans.

If the American Dream had one simple definition, it was that hard work led to a better life, materially and otherwise, if not for oneself then for one's children and grandchildren. In the late 1800s, when Horatio Alger published *Ragged Dick* and his other fictional chronicles of upward economic mobility, America's exceptionalism wasn't just a self-flattering myth. Back then a lot more Americans than people elsewhere really did move up the ladder from generation to generation. Our edge over Britain and the rest of Europe was diminishing by the 1950s, but economic mobility remained a real thing in the United States, onward and upward—until 1980.

That change is particularly clear in a recent study conducted by Stanford and Harvard economists. In 1970, they found, almost all thirty-year-old Americans, 92 percent, were earning more than their parents had at that age and older. Among Americans in their early thirties in 2012, however, only half were earning more than their parents had—and for sons compared to fathers, even fewer. That enormous difference over two generations was mainly caused not by slower economic growth, the economists found, but by how American economic growth was shared after 1980. If we'd continued slicing the pie as we'd done from 1940 until 1980, then 80 percent of those Gen-Xers would be earning more money than their Silent Generation parents, instead of only 50 percent.

These days, if you grow up poor in America, you have less than a one-in-four shot of becoming even solidly middle class—one in three if you're white, one in ten if you're black. If you grow up right in the economic middle, the chances are you won't move up at all. On the other hand, if you come from an upper-middle-class or rich household, the odds are strong you'll remain upper middle class or rich as an adult.

When inequality started increasing in the 1980s, separating the fortunate few and the unfortunate majority, it showed up geographically as well: not only were only the rich getting richer, but neighborhoods and cities and regions segregated accordingly. The economist Enrico Moretti calls this the Great Divergence. Before the 1980s, the decade in which gated communities became common, Americans tended to live more democratically. Americans with more money and less money were likelier to live alongside one another.

In 1970 only one in seven Americans lived in a neighborhood that was distinctly richer or poorer than their metropolitan area overall, but that fraction began growing in the 1980s, and by the 2000s it was up to a third. Before the 1980s, two-thirds of Americans lived in middle-income neighborhoods; now a minority of us do, a fact that makes the terms thrown around about the middle class—*disappeared, hollowed out*—seem less metaphorical.*

As the American middle class quickly grew from the 1940s to the '70s, so did economic equality—that is, the income gap between richer

---

*The good news is that while neighborhoods have gotten more economically homogeneous, they've also become more racially and ethnically diverse. In 1980 the residents of at least a quarter of all U.S. census tracts, each a neighborhood of a few thousand people, were essentially all white and non-Hispanic. Nowadays only 5 percent of white Americans live in such neighborhoods, most of them in rural areas.

and poorer steadily shrank. Interestingly, that same leveling also happened at the same time among *cities,* with wages back then growing faster in poorer places than they did in more affluent ones, allowing people in the laggard cities to catch up. But around 1980 that stopped too. Since then the average salary premiums for jobs in and around economically robust cities have grown to be several times as large as they'd been in the 1970s, tens of thousands of dollars a year more per employee instead of merely thousands. After 1980 college graduates with skills started getting paid less if they lived in and around Cleveland rather than thriving Omaha, or in Stockton rather than thriving San Jose, so they moved.

This Great Divergence is yet another way in which growing economic inequality gets built into the system and becomes self-perpetuating, with residents of richer cities and regions getting even richer while their fellow citizens in unfortunate places fall further behind.

Not only do people who live in Boston or Raleigh or Austin get to choose from better jobs, their wealth also increases more because of real estate prices, which have risen more than twice as fast in cities in general as in rural areas. Superhigh prices for apartments and houses, in turn, mean that it's harder for people from left-behind places to afford to migrate to booming urban areas, which is bad for them and probably for U.S. economic growth too. And people in the booming cities who aren't Internet workers or their masseuses have a much harder time affording to stay. In Seattle in the 1960s, for instance, a typical janitor and a typical lawyer both spent 10 or 15 percent of their incomes to live in an apartment or house they owned or rented; today the Seattle lawyer still pays 15 percent for housing, but the Seattle janitor has to pay around 40 percent.

One of my premises in this book is that a real and mainly good expression of American exceptionalism had been our willingness and eagerness to take on the *new.* That often meant pulling up stakes and hitting the road in search of new work or a new life. To be American was to be venturesome. In the heyday of the so-called American Century, in the 1940s, people were doing that in a big way. The percentage of people who lived in a state other than the one they were born in rose steeply, and it kept rising as the country boomed and became more equal—and then it stopped rising around, yes, 1980. Since then the rate at which people move to a new state or city for a new job has fallen by half, and it is now at the lowest it's been since the government began tracking it. People without